Hamilton's Campaign

with

Moore and Wellington

during the

Peninsular War

HAMILTON'S CAMPAIGN

WITH

MOORE AND WELLINGTON

DURING THE

PENINSULAR WAR

BY

SERGEANT ANTHONY HAMILTON

The Spellmount Library of Military History

SPELLMOUNT
Staplehurst

British Library Cataloguing in Publication Data:
A catalogue record for this book is available
from the British Library

Copyright © Spellmount 1998
Introduction © James Colquhoun 1998

ISBN 1-86227-017-1

First published in 1847

This edition first published in the UK in 1998
in
The Spellmount Library of Military History
by
Spellmount Limited
The Old Rectory
Staplehurst
Kent TN12 0AZ

1 3 5 7 9 8 6 4 2

Printed in Great Britain by
T.J. International Ltd
Padstow, Cornwall

AN INTRODUCTION
By James Colquhoun

In his book *Wellington's Army*, Sir Charles Oman commented on the considerable bulk of 'autobiographies and personal reminiscences which were written by participants in the war some time after it had come to an end – at any time from ten to forty years after 1814. Their name is legion. I am continuously discovering more of them printed obscurely in small editions and from local presses.' It is perhaps astonishing that since those words were written in 1912, these small volumes are still being discovered even now and Hamilton's history, published in upstate New York in 1847, is very much of this genre. It is, I believe, an honest, albeit sometimes rather quirky, attempt to describe the campaigns and battles in which he fought and suffered. It is though, the thread of his personal adventures which runs through the book which makes it so fascinating.

Hamilton was born and brought up in County Donegal on the west coast of Northern Ireland. He tells us that because his father died when he was young, he was bound to a trade. However he ran away and joined a recruiting party of the 43rd Light Infantry under the command of Lt Pollock. The implication is that he ran away when he was probably a teenager although I suspect though that he was actually in his mid-twenties when he joined the army. The clue to this is the fact that Lt Pollock was only commissioned as an Ensign in 1805. Regiments often sent recruiting parties to Ireland which was a constant source of good fighting men.

Hamilton finally went to Hythe in Kent to join his regiment. It is interesting to wonder if he was in the same intake which is described by an 'Anonymous Sergeant of the 43rd', who recalls that he found himself sharing a large barrack room with three companies of a hundred men each. 'They were chiefly volunteers, and of course young soldiers, many were Irish, many more were English, several Welshman were intermingled, and a few Scotch men came to complete the whole. Most of these, and that was the only point of general resemblance, had indulged in excessive drinking. Some were uproariously merry: on the others the effect was directly the reverse; and nothing less than a fight, it matter not with whom would satisfy.'

It is appropriate at this stage to comment on the regiment which Hamilton and his contemporaries had joined. It had been raised in 1741 as Thomas Fowke's Regiment of Foot and was redesignated the 43rd Regiment of Foot in 1751, adding the title Monmouthshire to it its title in 1782. In 1803 it had been selected to join a new Light Infantry Brigade and its proper title at this time, and indeed until 1881, was 43rd (The Monmouthshire) Regiment of Foot (Light Infantry). They had already seen active service at Quebec (1759), Martinique and Havana (1762) and in the American War of Independence (1775–1781). In the 1790s the regiment carried out two disastrous tours of the West Indies in which a large number of men died of fever.

By 1803 though, they were back at Shorncliffe near Hythe and brigaded with the 52nd (Light Infantry), 92nd Highlanders and the 95th Rifles under the command of Major General Sir John Moore. Moore's intention was to train his regiments to fight as individual skirmishers as well as being ordinary regiments of the line. This meant that every man had to be trained to use his initiative, to be quick and agile and to shoot straight. Drill movements were simplified and orders were transmitted by the bugle horn. The Light Brigade fought well at Copenhagen in 1806 under the command of Sir Arthur Wellesley.

Before we follow in Hamilton's footsteps and his version of the Peninsular War, it may help the reader to list the dates of the battles which he describes, especially as Hamilton omits them from to time. I have also marked those battles with an asterisk at which I believe he was present although, as we shall see, in two of them the 43rd was absent.

1809
Roliça, August 17. Vimiero*, August 21

1809
Corunna*, January 16. Oporto*, May 12. Talavera*, July 27 and 28

1810
Coa*, July 24. Busaco*, September 27

1811
Sabugal*, April 3. Fuentes d'Oñoro*, May 5. Albuera, May 16

1812
Ciudad Rodrigo*, January 19. Badajoz*, April 6. Salamanca*, July 22

1813
Vittoria*, June 21

1815
Quatre Bras, June 16. Waterloo, June 18

In August 1808 Sir Arthur Wellsley's expeditionary force consisted of the second battalion of the 43rd and at the battle of Vimiero it was involved in some of the severest fighting and proportionately lost more men than any other British battalion on that day. The 43rd lost 119 killed, wounded and missing which represents 16% of the overall total number of British casualties of 720.

The manoeuvres of the various armies leading up to the retreat to Corunna are not easy to follow without a detailed map. Nevertheless Hamilton's anecdotes describing some of the most harrowing events will only underline the frightfulness of those ghastly days. His story about the wife of Corporal Riley of the 42nd (misprint for 43rd?) Light Infantry who is drowned because she has so much bullion in her bloomers sounds as if it actually happened. Sir Henry Newbolt in his *Story of the Oxford and Buckinghamshire Light Infantry* repeats this story but says the wife of Maloney, the master Tailor of the 52nd, was the unfortunate lady! In his description of the battle of Corunna Hamilton states that he took part on the left wing of the British army under General Hope. If that was the case then I suspect that he had been separated from his battalion, which, being in Fraser's Division, was on the right wing and incidentally never fired a shot.

The idea that he had been separated from his battalion is given support by the fact that when we next hear about him Hamilton is charging up the main street of Oporto being cheered on by the local population on May 12th, 1809. The significance of this date is that neither the first nor second battalions of the 43rd were in Portugal at the time but were in fact still recruiting and recovering from the retreat to Corunna in their barracks in Colchester.

So how then did our hero find himself in Oporto? The answer must be that he had been cut off from his battalion at Corunna and somehow made his way down to Portugal. He was there reunited with at least 100 other stragglers from the 43rd who had recovered from their wounds and were all being placed together in a company of a composite battalion known as the Battalion of Detachments. There were two such battalions and the 43rd's company was in the first one in Stewart's Brigade.

Thus it is that we find Hamilton being badly wounded at Talavera on July 28th, 1809. He claims that he was part of Major General Cotton's Light Brigade. But since this brigade was composed of Light Cavalry, I find it hard to believe that Hamilton had become a cavalry man. I suspect his memory has played him tricks and he was still in Stewart's Brigade. He must have been enormously lucky to have survived that day, not only because he was nearly burnt to death, but also there were so many wounded (nearly 4,000) that it was estimated that two-thirds of the British army was involved in looking after them. Indeed, when Wellington was forced to retreat, he left 1,500 wounded behind in Talavera.

Since Hamilton jumps twelve months in his narrative we can only guess what happened to him. The British retreat to the Portuguese frontier lasted a month before they settled down into unhealthy cantonments near Badajoz. In September 1809 the Battalions of Detachments were sent back to their original units and the 43rd's company joined the first Battalion of the 43rd. This battalion which was part of Craufurd's Light Brigade had, after their celebrated forced march, joined the army just after the battle of Talavera.

In the ensuing months Wellington defended the frontiers of Portugal and on February 22nd, 1810 he expanded the Light Brigade by adding two battalions of Portuguese Chasseurs and renamed it the Light Division. This division under the energetic leadership of General Robert Craufurd was responsible for guarding 40 miles of frontier along two southern tributaries of the Duoro, the Coa and Aqueda, in the vicinity of Almeida. Thus it was that for once Craufurd under-estimated the situation and on July 24th, 1810 was nearly caught napping in a controversial action which Hamilton does not over-dramatise. After the fall of Almeida Wellington fell back on his prepared positions known as the Lines of Torres Vedras outside Lisbon. On the way back he fought the brilliant defensive battle of Busaco on September 27th, 1810. Hamilton's own account of this action is particularly interesting. The overwhelming charge made by a total of 1,800 bayonets of the 43rd and 52nd must have been terrifying. 'Great was the screetch set on foot by our fellows during the charge', wrote Lt Charles Booth of the 43rd afterwards.

And so the war rolls on backwards and forwards, with the Light Division always the first into action and the last out. In 1811 it acquitted itself particularly well at Sabugal and Fuentes d'Oñoro. But the highest point of its endeavours must be the storming of the great frontier fortresses of Ciudad Rodrigo and Badajoz in 1812. That Hamilton had volunteered to take part in the storming parties of both assaults speaks volumes for the man. But he was in good company. Eyewitnesses refer to the intense feelings of the men to do or die. Grattan of the 88th recalled that there was 'an indescribable something about their bearing' and 'a tiger-like expression of anxiety to fall upon their prey'. In both attacks the casualties were frightful. At Badajoz, the 43rd lost 20 officers and 334 men. Amongst these casualties was Lt-Col Macleod, aged 27, who was described by Wellington 'as an ornament to his profession' and was much loved by his men. Hamilton claims he was, with one other soldier, the only man left sober enough to dig his grave the next day. Later the officers arranged for a plaque in Macleod's memory to be erected in Westminster Abbey.

Finally Hamilton is captured on picket duty outside San Sebastian. We do not hear much about prisoners of war although there were many on both sides. Hamilton's experiences as a POW and his subsequent escape are therefore particularly interesting. He finally returns to the 2nd Battalion of the 43rd in England and seems almost immediately to have volunteered to join the York's Chasseurs based on the Isle of Wight. This regiment was mainly formed from deserters and was promptly sent out to the West Indies, only to be disbanded in 1819. Hamilton is right of course to thank his lucky stars that he did not rejoin the 1st/43rd who were so badly shot up in America in 1814. They finally sailed back to Belgium to arrive one day after the Battle of Waterloo; an episode of which presumably Hamilton was not aware.

In 1819 Hamilton was demobilised in Quebec where the 43rd had won its first battle honour exactly 60 years before. Like many professional soldiers both before and since, he found it difficult to settle down. He had a restless nature and was not attracted to the idea of becoming a farmer. He became instead an itinerant labourer digging the Utica Canal, imbibing a grog allowance of 7 gills or about a litre of spirits a day. It must have been a wonder that any work was done at all. Finally he is saved by a good woman (his mother-in-law!) and is converted to religion and the temperance movement.

I hope he died content. I would have loved to have met him to ask him all about the gaps in his story and much else. One really gets the impression he was almost indestructible. He was daring and brave and for all his fighting spirit he could show compassion. He had, I am sure, a sense of humour. To my mind Sergeant Anthony Hamilton is typical of the quintessentially professional infantryman who served in Wellington's army and fought for his regiment and his country with fearful, disciplined ferocity. He and his fellow veterans were truly invincible.

James Colquhoun
1998

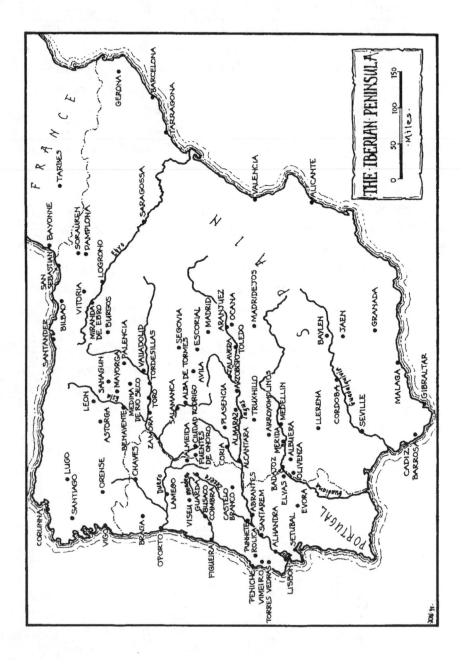

HAMILTON'S CAMPAIGN

WITH

MOORE AND WELLINGTON

DURING

THE PENINSULAR WAR.

ORIGINAL AND COMPILED.

PUBLISHED FOR THE AUTHOR.

TROY, N. Y.:

PRESS OF PRESCOTT & WILSON, CCXXV RIVER-STREET.

1847.

HAMILTON'S CAMPAIGN

WITH MOORE AND WELLINGTON.

At the request of a large circle of acquaintances and friends, as well as from my own choice, I offer to my numerous readers (as I hope they may be) a brief and unvarnished account of my humble life and adventures.

I was born on the 1st of January, 1779, in the town and parish of Raphoe, County of Donegall, in the North of Ireland.

My parents were much respected and were descendants of some of the first and best families that early settled in that part of the Island.

On my father's side I was a protestant, and on the part of my mother a catholic; suffice to say, the whole family went with mother to the mass, which left me a Roman Catholic.

My father had a good freehold property and was well to live; he died when I was quite young, which deprived me of the means of an early edu-

cation. I was bound out to a trade, but soon ran
away and went to Strabane in the county of Ty-
rone, where I enlisted in the 43d Light Infantry,
with Lieut. Pollock, who was afterwards wounded in the siege of Badajos.

We sailed from Warren's Point, recruits and all,
to Liverpool and went by the way of London, to
Kent.

We next sailed with an expedition from Hive
Barracks in Kent, to Copenhagen, in order to pun-
ish Denmark for going into an alliance with
France. We bombarded Copenhagen—the fleet
by water and the army by land. In this affair, I
was in the Light Brigade. We built sand-bank
batteries, drove in the advance piquet guards of
the Danish army, and captured the Danish fleet.
The consequence was, Denmark paid a heavy ran-
som to England to withdraw their armament.

We returned to England, and lay for a short
time in Barracks at Malden, in Essex.

Soon after the opening of the first campaign of
the British army destined for the Peninsula, we
sailed for Portugal and landed at Mondego Bay.
Previous to the landing of our division, Sir Arthur Wellesley, now the Duke of Wellington, left
Cork, Ireland, July 12th, 1808, with an army of
12,000 men, and landed at Mondego Bay, on the
1st of August. I was not present in this first engagement, but will give the details as received
from the most authentic and reliable sources.

BATTLE OF ROLICA.

On the 9th of August, the advanced guard of the army moved onward from the Mondego, by the way of Leiria, and on the 14th entered Alcobaca, from which the enemy had retired on the preceding night, and on the following day moved forward towards Caldas. At Brilos, a village in the neighborhood the first blood was shed. The post was attacked by some companies of riflemen of the 60th and 95th regiments, who carried it with trifling resistance on the part of the enemy, whom they incautiously pursued for several miles. The detachment however was in turn attacked by a superior force which endeavoured to cut off their retreat ; and it was only by the prompt assistance of General Spencer that this object was defeated. The loss of the British was 26 killed.

On the same day the army reached Caldas, and the advance, under Brigadier Gen. Fane, moved on to Obidos, and drove the enemy's piquets from the town. Gen. Delaborde, in the meantime, had retired to a position in front of Rolica. The heights on which this village is situated from the boundary of a valley commencing at Caldas and about three leagues in extent.

Nearly in the centre stand the town and old Moorish fort of Obidos ; and every favourable post on the high ground, on either side of the valley

1*

was occupied by detachments of the French army. The main body was posted on a plain, which overlooked the valley as far as Obidos.

On the morning of the 17th August, Sir Arthur Wellesley advanced to the attack. Columns were sent out on either flank; and on the approach of these, Delaborde, without offering resistance, fell back to the heights of Rolica, where he again placed his army in position.

The ground thus occupied was strong; and having been closely reconnoitered by Sir Arthur Wellesley, he made immediate preparation for attack. His army with this view was formed into three columns.

The right, consisting of twelve hundred Portuguese infanry, and fifty Portuguese cavalry, was intended to turn the left flank of the position, and penetrate into the mountains in the rear. The left consisting of Major General Ferguson's and Brigadier General Bowes' brigades of infantry, three companies of riflemen, and about forty cavalry, British and Portuguese, was destined under command of General Ferguson, to ascend the hills at Obidos, in order to turn the posts which the enemy still held on the left of the valley, as well as the right of his position at Rolica. The centre column, commanded by Sir Arthur in person, and consisting of Major General Hill's, Brigadier General Nightingale's, Crawford's and Fane's brigades, with four thousand Portuguese light infantry, and the main body of the British and Portuguese cavalry, was ordered to assemble in the plain, and attack the front of the position.

Such was the order of the attack. It was morning and a calm and quiet beauty seemed to linger on the scene of the impending conflict. The heights of Rolica, though steep and difficult of access possessed few of the sterner and more imposing features of mountain scenery. The heat and droughts of summer had deprived them of much of that brightness of verdure which is common in a colder and more variable climate. Here and there the face of the heights was indented by deep ravines, worn by the winter torrents, the precipitous banks of which were occasionally covered with wood; and below, extended groves of the cork tree and olive; while Obidos, with its ancient walls and fortress, and stupendous aqueduct, rose in the middle distance. To the east the prospect was terminated by the lofty summit of the Monte Junto, and on the west by the Atlantic.

As the centre column commenced its advance towards the steep acclivity in front, the enemy gave no demonstration of hostility; and all was still and peaceful, as when the goat-herd tended his flock on the hilly pastures, and the peasant went forth to his labours, carolling his matin song in the sunrise. Such was the scene about to be consecrated in the eyes of posterity by the first

considerable outpouring of British blood, in a cause
as pure, just, noble, and generous, as any of which
history bears record.

The position of the enemy could only be approached in front by narrow paths, winding through deep
and rocky ravines, and surrounded by masses of
brushwood, in which Delaborde had stationed his
light infantry. Till reaching the bottom of the
heights, the British troops were protected by the
cork and olive woods from the fire of the enemy's
artillery. But in their ascent, the troops had to
encounter a resistance, which became at every
stage of their progress more fierce and vehement.
A heavy fire was opened on the assailants from
the brush-wood on either flank, and at every point
at which they became exposed to the action of artillery, a shower of cannon-shot came sweeping
down the ravines with terrible effect.

Even in these difficult and disheartening circumstances, no symptoms of confusion were man-
ifested in the British columns. The advance of
General Nightingale's brigade was led by the 29th
regiment, with singular bravery and resolution.
They beheld themselves suffering from attacks
which it was impossible to repel; but the high discipline of the regiment enabled it to surmount
every obstacle; and, under every disadvantage,
they kept on their way steady and unbroken. The
Honorable Lieutenant-Colonel Lake, by whom

it was commanded fell, as the head of the column reached the sumit of the hill, and became exposed to a heavy and destructive fire from the vineyards occupied by the enemy. The grenadier company of the twenty-ninth were in the act of forming, when a French battalion after pouring in a volley, advanced to the charge, and succeeded in over-powering the small but gallant body, which had already crowned the heights. This success was temporary. The remainder of the regiment, came up, and supported by the ninth regiment, the colonel of which was also killed, they drove back the enemy, and succeeded in maintaining their position, against every effort to regain possession of the heights.

The success thus gallantly achieved was rendered more decided by the brigade of General Hill which had already formed on the heights, and the appearance of the column of General Ferguson, which at first had taken a wrong direction, but was now observed to be traversing the right flank of the enemy's position. Delaborde's situation had now become one of extreme peril; and he was too skillful a general not at once to perceive the necessity of immediate retreat. Precipitately abandoning his position, he retired to the village of Zambugeira, where he again made demonstration of resistance. From this by a most gallant charge, he was driven by General Spencer.

The loss of the French, in this engagement, was six hundred killed and wounded and among the latter of which was their brave and skilful leader. That on our side was somewhat less.

BATTLE OF VIMIERO.

The next battle in order is that of Vimicro fought on the 21st of August 1808. In this battle I was actively engaged.

Delaborde driven from the village of Zambugeira, retired with his army, by the road to Torres Vedras. It was the intention of Sir Arthur Wellesley to have lost no time in following the enemy; but having learned that our re-inforcement under General Acland had arrived and was in the offing, he changed his resolution, and moved onward by the coast road in order to cover our landing and receive supplies from the shipping.

Our division and the brigade under General Anstruther now joined Wellington's troops and expected every hour to meet the enemy.

Early on the morning of the 21st August, Sir Arthur Wellesley visited the advanced posts, but could discern no sign of an approaching enemy. About seven o'clock, however, a cloud of dust was observed in the extremity of the horizon, slowly moving in the direction of our army, and at eight o'clock, a strong body of the enemy's cavalry was observed on the heights to the southward. In a

short time a strong column of infantry appeared
on the road from Torres Vedras to Lourinha ; and
it became evident that we must come to a general
engagement.

The village of Vimiero stands in a valley, wa-
tered by the little rivulet Maceira, at the eastern
extremity of a high mountainous range, which ex-
tends westward to the sea. In front of the village
is a hill of inferior altitude, terminating in a plateau of considerable extent, and commanded from
several points. On the left is another strong ridge
of heights, stretching to the eastward, and terminating on the right in a deep ravine. Over these
heights passes the road to Lourinha, through the
villages of Fontanel and Ventoso.

Such were the more prominent features of the
ground. It was thus occupied by Sir Arthur Wellesley ; six brigades were stationed on the mountain to the westward of the village. The advanced guard, under General Fane, and the brigade of
General Anstruther, with six pieces of artillery,
occupied the plateau. The cavalry and reserve of
artillery were posted in the valley between the
heights, ready to support the troops on the plateau,
should that part of the position be attacked. The
Lourinha road was guarded by the Portuguese
troops and a small body of riflemen. The ground
having been taken up on the previous evening,
rather with a view to temporary convenience than

military defence, a piquet only had been stationed
on the ridge to the westward.   As it was obvious,
however, from the enemy's demonstrations, that
the left and centre were about to become the chief
theatres of conflict, the brigades of Generals Ferguson, Nightingale, Acland, and Bowes, were successively moved from the mountain on the west
to the heights on the Lourinha road, in order to
strengthen what was evidently the most vulnera-
ble part of the position.

At nine o'clock the action commenced.   Juniot
had formed his army in two divisions.   The first
of these, consisting of about six thousand men,
was commanded by General Delaborde.   The second, under Loison, was nearly equal in amount.
The reserve, composed of four battalions of grenadiers, was commanded by General Kellerman, and
acted as a connecting link between the two principal divisions.   The cavalry under General Margaron, was stationed partly in rear of the reserve,
and partly on the right of Delaborde's division.

The two divisions continued their advance,
across the rough and wooded country in front of
the position towards the plateau in the centre.   On
approaching the scene of action, however each
division, separated into several minor columns,
which commenced nearly simultaneous attacks on
different portions of the British line.   The most
vehement was that headed by Delaborde in per-

son, who first came in contact with the brigade of General Anstruther, which occupied the left of the plateau, and the village of Vimiero. During its advance, this body was exposed to a destructive fire of artillery, which it bore with great steadiness and gallantry, and rapidly forced back the skirmishers who had been stationed in the woods on either flank. A check, however, was soon given to the progress of the assailants, who having reached the summit of the plateau, were met by a destructive volley from the fiftieth regiment, which afterwards rushed on to the charge, and drove them in confusion and with great slaughter, down the face of the hill. The attack on General Fane's brigade was no less decisively repulsed; and a regiment, which was advancing on the village, by the church, was opportunely attacked in flank by the brigade of General Acland, then moving to its position on the heights. A most gallant charge by the small body of cavalry led by Colonel Taylor, completed the discomfiture of the enemy in this quarter. They fled in utter confusion, and were vigorously pursued by Colonel Taylor and his squadron, for nearly two miles; when General Margaron, who commanded the French cavalry, observing the small number of the assailants, advanced to the charge; and the remnant of this brave band were compelled to retreat, with the loss of their leader. General

Kellerman having rallied the fugitives, made a last effort with the reserve to retrieve the fortunes of the day. A column strongly supported by artillery, was again sent forward to gain possession of the village of Vimerio.

Here our regiment, the 43d. was posted, close by the road that entered the village. The enemy advanced upon us with determination and valor, but after a desperate struggle on our part, were driven back with great slaughter. It was not only a hot day but also a hot fight, and one of our men by the name of McArthur, who stood by me, having opened his mouth to catch a little fresh air, a bullet from the enemy at that moment entered his mouth obliquely, which he never perceived, until I told him his neck was covered with blood. He, however, kept the field until the battle was over. No farther attempt was made by the enemy on our position; and they retired, leaving seven pieces of artillery, and a great number of prisoners in our possession.

While these events were passing in the centre, an attack, no less resolutely supported, was made on the left of our army, which occupied the heights, on the Lourinha road. In that quarter Gen. Ferguson, whose brigade had been moved from the right to the left of the line, had scarcely taken up his ground, when he found himself assailed by a strong body of cavalry and infantry. The engagement was fierce, and resolutely maintained on both sides. The troops of Ferguson remained immoveable under every effort to dislodge them; and, on the coming up of the eighty-second and twenty-ninth regiments, the enemy were charged with the bayonet, and driven back in confusion. The French cavalry endeavoured to retrieve the misfortune of the infantry by several charges, but in vain. They were uniformly repulsed with unshaken steadiness, by the brigades of Ferguson and Nightingale, and at length ceased from farther attack.

The fruit of this achievement was the capture of six guns; and General Ferguson, leaving the seventy-first and eighty-second regiments to guard these honorable trophies, was in full pursuit of the discomfited enemy, when the brigade of Brenier, suddenly emerging from the ravine, attacked the two battalions, and for a moment, succeeded in retaking the captured artillery. But the regiments instantly rallied; and by a desperate charge with the bayonet, at once drove back the brigade of Brenier into the ravine, and remained masters of the guns. In this charge, General Brenier was made prisoner.

Affairs were in this situation on the left, when General Ferguson received an unexpected order to desist from the pursuit. In this crisis of the battle, Sir Harry Burrard arrived on the field, who from what motive I am unable to say; declined the responsibility of command, till the enemy were repulsed. As soon as the corps of Gen. Ferguson halted, in compliance with the command of Sir Harry Burrard, the enemy taking advantage, were rallied by General Thiebault, and withdrawn, under the protection of the cavalry, to a position in rear of Toledo.

Sir Arthur Wellesley naturally anxious to reap the full fruit of his victory, represented to his superior in command, the importance of following up with vigour, the advantages already gained, and others likely to follow, but to this measure, Sir Harry refused his compliance. It is reported, that Sir Arthur Wellesley, having, in vain, used used every argument and persuasion to change the determination of his leader, was heard to say, on retiring from the conference, " well then, we have nothing to do but go and shoot red-legged par tridges," the game with which that country abounds.

The results of this brilliant victory were the capture of a general officer and several hundred men, thirteen pieces of cannon, and twenty three waggons loaded with ammunition. The total loss of the enemy, in battle, has been estimated at three thousand. The French fought with great bravery, each man receiving a crown, and a pint of brandy as a reward to drive us into the sea.

On the morning after the battle, Sir Hew Dalrymple landed in Marceira Bay, and assumed the command of the army, which still remained on the field of Vimerio. In the course of the day a large body of French cavalry was observed approaching our outposts, and the whole line was immediately ordered under arms. The object of the enemy, however, was pacific, and the cavalry was soon ascertained to constitute the escort of General Kellerman, who came with a flag of truce. After due deliberation among the generals an arimistice was concluded.

After the convention and arimistice of Cintra, by which it was agreed, under certain regulations that the French army should evacuate Portugal, Sir John Moore was appointed Commander of the Peninsular army.

The agreement of Cintra tarnished the glory of the British arms and was disapproved of by the English Cabinet.

The French, on leaving, plundered the churches, public Libraries and Cabinets, and carried away much private and public property.

On the liberation of Portugal, it was determined by the British government to despatch an expedition to the north of Spain. Preparations for this purpose were immediately set on foot by Sir Hugh Dalrymple and Sir Harry Burrard without any considerable progress being made in the equipment of the army for active service.

On the 6th of October 1808. Sir John Moore received official information of his being appointed to command the troops destined for the Peninsula. The officer commanding the forces in Portugal was directed to detach a corps of twenty thousand infantry, with two regiments of German light cavalry, and a suitable body of artillery, to be placed under his orders, and that this force would be joined by a corps of ten thousand men then assembling at Falmouth, under command of Sir David Baird.

Sir John Moore was instructed to proceed with the troops under his more immediate command without any avoidable delay; and was instructed to fix on some place of rendezvous, for the whole army either in Gallicia or on the borders of Leon. The specific plan of future operations, he was to concert with the commanders of the Spanish armies. Few effective preparations had been made for the equipment of the troops by his predecessors in command. Magazines were to be formed, and means of transport to be provided, in an impoverished and exhausted country. The approach of the rainy season, rendered it above all things desirable, that the army should, as soon as possible set forward on its march. These formidable difficulties were, however overcome by Moore; and in less than a fortnight from the period of his assuming the command, the greater part of the army was on its march to the frontier.

It formed part of the instructions of the government, that the cavalry should proceed by land; but a discretionary power was vested in the commander to move the infantry by sea or land, as he might judge most advisable. Sir John Moore preferred the latter, because, at that season of the year, a coasting voyage was uncertain and precarious; and because he was informed that, at Corunna, there were scarcely means of equipment for the force under Sir David Baird, already destined for that port.

Considerable difficulties occurred in ascertaining the state of the roads; and, deceived by erroneous information on that point, Sir John Moore determined on dividing his army, a dangerous arrangement, and one by which the period of concentration would of necessity be retarded. In consequence of this decision, the troops were ordered to march in three columns.

A corps of six thousand men, composed of the cavalry, four brigades of artillery, and four regiments of infantry, under command of Lieutenant-General Hope, were directed to pass through the Alentejo, and proceed by the route of Badajos, Merida, Truxillo, Talavera de La Reyna, and the Escurial.

Three brigades, commanded by Major-General Fraser, marched by Abrantes and Almeida.

Two brigades commanded by Major-General

Beresford, were sent by Coimbra and Almeida. As it was deemed imprudent, by Sir John Moore, that the two latter columns should be without artillery, a brigade of light six-pounders was likewise directed on Almeida.

The different corps of the army having commenced their march, Sir John Moore quitted Lisbon on the twenty-seventh of October. On the eighth of November he was at Almeida. On the thirteenth he arrived at Salamanca, where he received intelligence of the defeat and dispersion of Belvidere's army before Burgos. This event seems to have inspired the British general with melancholy foreboding of the fate of the contest in which he was about to engage.

On the second night after his arrival, he was awakened by an express from General Pignatelli conveying intelligence that the enemy had pushed on a body of cavalry to Valladolid, a city not above three marches from Salamanca.

The situation of Sir John Moore had thus suddenly become one of extreme peril. The enemy were in his front; and he had in Salamanca only three brigades of infantry, and not a single gun.

In these circumstances, he contemplated again retiring on Portugal. He assembled the Junta of Salamanca; and laying before them the information he had received, stated, that should the enemy continue their advance on his front—now wholly

uncovered—the British army had no option but
retreat. On the arrival of intelligence, however
that the French troops had been withdrawn to
Palencia, he determined on continuing his head
quarters at Salamanca; and directed Generals
Baird and Hope to close on that city with their
divisions.

Every day brought with it intelligence of fresh
disasters, By the battle of Espinosa, Blake's army
had been dispersed. The whole left wing of the
Spanish army, which occupied a line reaching from
Bilboa to Burgos, had thus been annihilated; and
the flank of the centre, under Castanos, was laid
open to the enemy.

The situation of Sir John Moore at Salamanca,
with respect to the Spanish armies, was very extraordinary. He was at the vertex of a triangle,
the base of which, at the distance of between two
hundred and fifty, and three hundred miles, was
the French position,—the points at the extremities
of the base, that is the French flanks, were the positions of the Spanish armies,

The army of Castanos was at this period posted
in the neighbourhood of Tudela, but on the opposite or north side of the Ebro, and about three hundred miles to the north-east of Salamanca. The
French were thus completely interposed between
the Spanish and British armies; and might, at
any moment, advance on the latter in overwhelm-

ing force. For this state of things Sir John Moore was unprepared. All his arrangements had been framed on the assurance that the assembling of his forces would be protected by the Spanish armies. To effect the union of his isolated divisions had now become an operation of danger and difficulty. The position of these bodies was such as to prevent the possibility of immediate action. He was placed as a central point between the two wings of his army, and found it impracticable to approach the one, without hazarding the safety of the other.

Thus compelled to remain inactive at Salamanca. Sir John Moore endeavoured to stimulate the local authorities into the adoption of such measures of promptitude and vigour as were suited to the exigence of the crisis. In this effort he failed. The Spanish people, though still influenced by fierce and unmitigated hatred of their invaders, were no longer animated by that uncalculating and convulsive energy which, in the commencement of the struggle, had goaded them like madness into furious resistance. The fierceness of the paroxism had passed; and though, in the cause of their country, the hand of every Spaniard was prepared to gripe the sword, the blows it dealt were directed with an erring aim and by a feeble arm. Their detestation of a foreign yoke was undiminished; but it had become a fixed and inert sentiment, rather than a fierce, uncontrollable, and all-prevailing impulse.

Before entering Spain, every thing had contributed to conceal the real state of the Peninsula
from the penetrating vision of Sir John Moore.
The British government, itself deceived, had become, in its turn, the involuntary propagator of
deception.   At the commencement of the struggle,
it had dispatched military agents to the head-quarters of the different Spanish generals, to act as
organs of communication, and transmit authentic
intelligence of the progress of events in the seat of
war. The persons selected for this service were,
generally, officers undistinguished by talent or experience, and therefore little suited to discharge
with benefit, the duties of an office so delicate and
important.   They seem generally to have become
the dupes of the unwarranted confidence and in-
flated boasting of those by whom they were surrounded; and their reports were framed in a strain
of blind and sanguine anticipation, not deducible
from any enlarged or rational view of the prospects
or condition of the people.   Instead of true repre-
sentations of the numbers, character, and state of
efficiency of the armies, they were deluded into
adopting the extravagant hyperboles of rash and
vain-glorious men, and contributed what in them
lay to propagate false and exaggerated notions of
the military power of the Spanish nation.   They
did not venture to obtrude on the British Cabinet
the unpalatable truth that the national army was
in effect, nothing more than a congregation of

separate and independent bands miserably armed, possessing but a scanty and ill-served artillery, and almost destitute of cavalry. Had they done so; and had they stated likewise, that this army was without magazines of any kind, without generals of talent or experience, without officers sufficiently versed in the details of war, to instruct and discipline the raw levies which constituted the greater part of its numerical strength, and, further, that the different leaders were prevented by frivolous jealousies, and discordance of opinion, from cordially uniting in the execution of any great operation, the calamitous events on the Ebro would probably not have come like a thunderbolt to crush and stultify the combinations of a government, which was at least sincerely anxious to co-operate in the cause of freedom.

England had furnished Spain with supplies; she had poured arms and munitions into the country with a profuse hand; but she had taken no efficacious measures for their judicious application. She exercised little influence on the counsels of the Spanish government; and even while providing the very thews and sinews of the war her voice was seldom listened to with obedience or respect. Arms, placed at the disposal of men swayed by petty views and local interests, were wasted and misapplied; and the supplies of money, clothing, and ammunitions, so liberally afforded, became a

bone of contention and of petty jealousy to the
rival authorities. In truth, the provincial govern-
ors were actuated by no liberal and enlarged
views of the public benefit. Supine in danger,
and vain-glorious in prosperity, at once untalent-
ed and unenlightened, no men could be more un-
fitted to direct the resources of a nation with vigour and effect.

In such men Sir John Moore could place no
trust. His expectations had been deceived. He
found supineness where he expected energy; a
people not filled with an active spirit—stirring en-
thusiasm, but reposing in a dull, immovable, and
lethargic confidence in their own prowess and
resources, even in the immediate neighbourhood
of a triumphant enemy. His mind became not
only perplexed but irritated by the disappointment
of his hopes. At Salamanca he knew himself to
be placed in a difficult and precarious position, un-
protected in front, separated from the wings of his
army, with nothing but a barren country to retire
upon. To the concentration of his forces, he was
aware, indeed, that no present obstacle existed;
but how long such a state of things might continue, he had no data on which to form a judg-
ment. The enemy at any moment might inter-
pose a body which would prevent the possibility
of a junction, for there existed no Spanish force
from which he could anticipate protection.

To the other embarrassments of Sir John Moore must be added, the difficulty of receiving true and faithful intelligence of the events passing around him. On public and official reports no confidence could be placed, and of more authentic sources of intelligence he was in a great measure deprived. He had been sent forward without a plan of operations, or any data on which to found one. Castanos was the person with whom he had been directed to concert his measures; but that officer had been superseded by Romana; and of the situation of the latter, Sir John Moore only knew that he was engaged in rallying the remains of Blake's army, at a distance of about two hundred miles. Naturally distrustful of the apocryphal intelligence transmitted by the British military residents, he could rely only on the reports of Colonel Graham and Captain Whittingham; and these, in conjunction with the information which his own officers were enabled to procure, contributed still further to deepen the gloom by which his mind was overcast.

It was in such circumstances and under the influence of such feelings, that Sir John Moore wrote to Mr. Frere, the new minister at Madrid, whose opinions he had been instructed to receive with deference and attention, proposing as a question what course he should pursue, in case the army of Castanos, which yet shewed front to the enemy, should be defeated. Should that event occur, "I must," said Sir John Moore, in a letter dated twenty-seventh November, "either march upon Madrid, and throw myself into the heart of Spain, and thus run all risks, and share the fortunes of the Spanish nation; or I must fall back on Portugal. In the latter case, I fall back upon my resources, upon Lisbon; cover a country where there is British interest; act as a diversion in favor of Spain, if the French detach a force against me; and am ready to return to the assistance of the Spaniards, should circumstances again render it eligible."

On the day following the date of this communication, intelligence arrived for which Sir John Moore was certainly not unprepared. Castanos had been defeated at Tudela with great loss, and the road to Madrid was now open to the French armies. In this state of things, without waiting for the answer of Mr. Frere, Sir John Moore determined on immediate retreat. With this intention, he transmitted orders to Sir David Baird at Astorga, and Sir John Hope at the Escurial. The former of these officers was directed to retire on Corunna, the latter to push forward if possible to Salamanca. Sir David Baird was likewise directed to write immediately to England, that a supply of transports might be sent to the Tagus. "They will be wanted," said Sir John Moore; "for when the French have Spain, *Portugal cannot be defended.*"

Having thus formed his decision, the commander-in-chief directed a council of General Officers to assemble at head-quarters. He laid before them a full statement of the intelligence he had received and made known the resolution which it had induced him to adopt. His tone was manly and decided. He informed the generals that he had not called them together to request their counsel, or to influence them to commit themselves by giving any opinion on the course he had determined to pursue. He took the responsibility entirely upon himself, and he onl · required that they would immediately take measures for carrying the plan into effect.

When the resolution of their General was made known to the army, it was received by all ranks with more than murmurs of dissatisfaction and disgust. The British army had suffered no disaster; it had never been brought into contact with the enemy; and all felt that to retreat with untried prowess from the scene of contest would fix a tarnish on our arms, and, by diminishing the confidence of the Spanish nation in our zeal and devotion to their cause, would proportionally contribute to strengthen and consolidate the power of the usurper. All lamented the order for retreat—all felt that it must cast a blight on that cause which they were prepared to defend by the outpouring of their blood. In his reply to the letter of Sir John Moore, Mr. Frere protested strongly against the measure of retiring on Portugal. He assured him it was one most deprecated by the Spanish government. He urged the expediency of advancing to co-operate in the defence of Madrid by every argument in his power. "Of the zeal and energy of the people," said Mr. Frere, " I have no doubt." &c.

The arguments of Mr. Frere did not succeed in changing the opinions of Sir John Moore. He still adhered to the resolution he had previously formed and only awaited the arrival of Sir John Hope to commence his retreat on Portugal.

Sir John Moore, however on receiving further information from Mr. Frere decided on a change of plan, and accordingly sent orders to Sir David Baird to make arrangements for returning to Astorga, and that combined efforts might be made for the support of Madrid, as that city had refused to capitulate to the French.

On the 12th of December, Sir John Moore moved onward from Salamanca and fixed his head quarters at Toro. He had now resolved, if possible to attack Marshal Soult at Saldanha, about eighty miles to the northward of Toro.

On the 18th of December, our army moved forward to Castro Nuevo, and on the twentieth, the junction with Sir David Baird was formed at Mayorga. The total effective amount of the combin-

ed army is stated to have been twenty three thous-
and infantry, and two thousand seven hundred
cavalry.

About one thousand seven hundred men were
on detachment, and four thousand in hospital.

While head-quarters were at Mayorga, several
skirmishes took place between the British cavalry
and that of the enemy. In Sahagun a detachment
of seven hundred French cavalry was reported to
be lodged, and Lord Paget deemed it practicable
to cut them off. The ground was covered with
deep snow and the weather intensely cold. Lord
Paget however set forward on his march, and de-
taching General Slade with the tenth hussars a-
long the sea to enter the town, he wheeled off with
the fifteenth and the horse-artillery to approach it
by a different route. By day-dawn Lord Paget
had reached the town, in front of which he fell in
with a picquet of the enemy. It was instantly
charged, and all but one man cut down or made
prisoners. The escape of this individual however
gave the alarm; and before the fifteenth could advance, the enemy were discerned drawn up to receive them in an open plain.

Lord Paget immediately formed line and advanced to the charge. But the success of this manœuvre was prevented by a broad ditch or ravine,
hitherto unobserved, which obstructed their progress. Some manœuvring took place between the
corps, each endeavoring to gain the flank of the

other. By superior skill Lord Paget at length effected his object. The ravine was passed, and,
coming down at full speed on their opponents, the
fifteenth overthrew them in a moment. Many of
the French were killed and one hundred and fifty
seven prisoners including two lieutenant-colonels,
were brought back to the British camp as trophies
of success. The loss of the fifteenth in this engagement was trifling.

On the 21st of December, our army moved to
Sahagun, where Sir John Moore halted for a day
to afford refreshment to the troops.

There he received a despatch from Romana, dated, Leon, December 19th. The Marquess expressed his approbation of the measures of Sir John
Moore, and his willingness to co-operate in his
proposed attack on Soult. But the most extraordinary feature in the letter is, that the writer of it
appeared wholly ignorant of the surrender of Madrid, nearly twenty days before! Another letter received on the day following stated that Soult, apprehensive of attack, had applied for re-inforcements ; and, in the meanwhile had collected the
nearest troops which had augmented his force to
about eighteen thousand men. These he had posted behind the Carrion. In the proposed operation,
Romana offered to unite with nine or ten thousand
of his best men, and intimated his readiness to advance immediately on receiving the answer of Sir
John Moore. This letter arrived late on the night

of the 22d December. Early on the following
morning Sir John Moore despatched a messenger
to Romana informing him that he would on the
same night, march to the town of Carrion, where
he had reason to believe that a body of the enemy
were collected.

"To-morrow" said the General; "I shall march
on Saldanha. If your Excellency would march
from Mansilla, either direct on Saldanha, or pass
the river a little above it, whilst I march on from
Carrion, I think it would distract the attention of
the enemy and considerably aid my attack. My
march from Carrion will probably be in the night.
Any information of your movemonts I shall thank
you to address me at Carrion where I shall be at
daylight to-morrow." In consequence of this determination, orders for an immediate advance were
issued to the army. The march was to commence
at eight o'clock in the evening, in two columns.
One of these was destined to force the bridge at
Carrion, and so penetrate to Saldanha; and this
body was already on the road, when a letter arrived from Romana, stating that the French, on the
side of Madrid, were in motion to the northward.
This intelligence co-incided with the information
received by Sir John Moore from other quarters.
The corps of the enemy, which was directing its
march to Badajos, had halted at Talavera. Large
supplies of forage and provisions had been ordered in the villages around Palencia. It was said

that Napoleon himself had set out from Madrid, with the avowed intention of proceeding to Bene-vente, without a halt. Under these circumstances Sir John Moore determined on retreat and the march to Carrion was countermanded. He con-sidered that the beneficial object of his movement had already been obtained. The progress of the enemy's armies had been arrested in the south, and they were now advancing on all hands to sur-round him. Sir John Moore, therefore, felt con-vinced, that nothing but immediate retreat could extricate him from the difficulties of his situation. His intentions were communicated to the Marques de la Romana in the following words, " I shall take immediate measures for retiring on Astorga. There I shall stand ; as my retreat thence, if ne-cessary, will be secure, I shall be in the way to re-ceive the supplies and the re-inforcements which I expect from England.   At the worst, I can main-tain myself, and, with your Excellency's aid de-fend the Gallicias, and give time for the forma-tion of the armies in the south, and that which you command, to be prepared, when a joint effort may be made, which can alone be efficacious." As Sir John Moore had not yet resigned the inten-tion of defending Gallicia, he determined on retir-ing in such a direction as would facilitate the ex-ecution of this measure, should it be found desira-ble.   To effect this, it was necessary in the first

instance to cross the Eslar, which could be done
by three routes. The first is by Mansilla where
the river is crossed by a bridge. The second
by Valencia de San Juan at which point there
is a ferry. The third is by Castro Gonzalo where
there is likewise a bridge, and from whence a road
passes to Benevente. As Mansilla was already occupied by the Spanish troops, the two
latter routes were preferred, and Astorga was
indicated as the place of rendezvous, where it was
understood the army would make a stand. In the
meanwhile Romana was expected to keep possession of Mansilla, and defend the city of Leon to the
last extremity. The day following was employed
In preparations for retreat. In the evening Gen.
Hope, with his own division and that of Gen. Frazer, fell back to Mayorga, and Sir David Baird retired to Valencia de San Juan. To conceal this
movement strong patrols of cavalry were pushed
on to the advanced posts of the enemy. On the
25th the Commander-in-Chief followed Gen. Hope
with the reserve and two light brigades. Lord
Paget was ordered to remain with the cavalry until evening, and then to follow the reserve. Much
difficulty was anticipated by Sir John Moore in
crossing the Eslar, from the melting of the mountain snows; but, on the 26th December, Sir David
Baird reached that river and crossed it with trifling
impediment. The other divisions of the army pro-

ceeded, without molestation, to Castro Gonzalo.
At this moment our army had become almost gird-
led by the enemy. From the 22d to the 24th,
Soult had received strong reinforcements—and his
army alone was already superior in numbers to the
British. Junot, with the army liberated by the
convention of Cintra had advanced from Burgos
to Palencia, and threatened their right flank. Napoleon in person had set out from Madrid with all
the disposable force in that quarter ; and on the
same day that the van of the British quitted Sahagun, the advanced guard of this army passed
through Tordesillas, a town about fifty miles distant from Benevente. The corps of Lefebore had
changed the direction of its march, and was now
advancing on Salamanca. The retreat of the
British army on Portugal was thus cut off. The
whole disposable force of the enemy, forming an
irregular crescent were thus advancing in *radii*
on the British army as a common centre. To cut
off its retreat was now the chief object of Napoleon. On the 26th, an engagement took place between the British cavalry and that of the enemy.
Detachments from the army of Napoleon had been
pushed on to Villalpando and Mayorga ; and in
the neighborhood of the latter place, a considerable force of the enemy was observed to be drawn
up on the acclivity of a hill, with the view apparently of cutting off any stragglers who might wan-

der from the line of march. Two squadrons of the
tenth Hussars were instantly ordered to dislodge
them. These under the command of Col. Leigh
rode gallantly up the hill, and by a successful
charge drove back the French cavalry in confusion. In this affair many of the enemy were killed
and wounded, and above one hundred made prisoners. On the same day, the cavalry, the horse-artillery, and a brigade of light-infantry, halted at
Castro Gonzalo ; and the divisions under Generals
Hope and Frazer marched to Benevente. On the
27th the rear guard crossed the Eslar, and followed the same route, having blown up the bridge.
The hardships to which the army were now exposed, tended greatly to increase the general feeling of dissatisfaction at the measures of their leader. The route lay over miserable roads, and
through an exhausted country. The weather was
more than usually severe ; heavy showers of rain
and sleet drenched the soldiers to the skin, and it
was not always even at night, that they could procure shelter from the elements.—Turbulence and
insubordination broke forth in the ranks. The
soldiers indignant at the Spaniards, who generally
locked their doors on their approach, and concealed their little stock of provisions, were guilty of
violence and robbery. These criminal excesses increased the evil. Hatred and disgust sprang up
on both sides, and frequent scenes of bloodshed

were the consequence. On the 27th December, the army reached Benevente ; and Sir John Moore issued a general order, characterising its excesses in strong language. He expressed his deep regret, that the army should have forfeited its former praise for exemplary conduct and discipline.

From Benevente, Sir John Moore dispatched a courier to Romana, informing him that the enemy were in full advance, and, that on the preceding day, their main body had reached Valladolid, one three marches to the rear. While at Benevente, where the army halted for two days, intelligence was received that Napoleon was endeavoring by forced marches to overtake the British. Under these circumstances, Sir John Moore hastened to continue his retreat. The stores of the army, for which no transport could be procured were ordered to be destroyed, and among the rest, kegs containing dollars were staved and rolled down a steep into the snow. The wife of Corporal Riley of the 42d Light-infantry, so loaded herself with the money that was scattered about, that afterwards, when embarking in Corunna harbor, in trying to get up into the vessel, she had such a weight around her person, that she fell between the boat and ship, and was drowned.

From Benevente to Vigo, there are two roads, one passing by Orense, the other by Astorga. The former though the shortest, was impracticable for

artillery, and the army were consequently compelled to retire by the latter. Orders were sent
to Sir David Baird, who was still at Valencia, to
continue his march on Astorga. On the 28th, Gens.
Hope and Frazer proceeded with their divisions to
La Banessa. On the 29th, Sir John Moore followed with the reserve ; and Lord Paget was directed
to bring up the rear with the cavalry. The march
of the cavalry however had not yet commenced,
when a body of the enemy's horse was observed to
be attempting a ford near the ruins of the bridge,
which had been blown up ; and presently between five and six hundred of the Imperial Guard
plunged into the river and crossed over. They
were instantly opposed by the piquets under Col.
Otway, which had been appointed to act as a rear-
guard. Though this body mustered little more
than two hundred men, they boldly advanced
against the enemy, and continued bravely to dis-
pute every inch of his advance. Repeated charges
took place between the front squadrons ; and upon the arrival of a small party of the 3d dragoons,
the front squadron, by a furious charge, broke
through that of the enemy and were for a time
surrounded. By another charge however, they
soon extricated themselves, and reformed with the
rest of the detachments. Lord Paget soon reached
the field, and Brig. Gen. Stewart assuming the
command of the piquets, made repeated charges

on the enemy, who were soon repulsed and fled in
great disorder to the river, closely pursued, leaving fifty-five killed and wounded on the field and
seventy prisoners, among whom was Gen. Lefeb-
vre, the commander of the Imperial guard. Our
loss in this affair amounted to about fifty, killed
and wounded.

On the day following, our head-quarters were at
Astorga, where Sir David Bairds' column, coming
from Valencia, succeeded in effecting a junction
with the main body of the army. At Astorga, another disappointment awaited Sir John Moore.
He found the city occupied by five thousand of the
corps of Romana. This General had not destroyed the bridge of Mansilla. The guard he left there
was driven back by a party of the enemy's cavalry. At Leon no defence had been attempted, and
the unexpected presence of the Spanish army at
Astorga, interfered materially with the arrangements of Sir John Moore. It had been his opinion
that Romana would have most contributed to the
good of the common cause, by retiring on the As-
turias; because when the enemy proceeded to
Gallicia, he might have intercepted their convoys,
or have compelled them to employ large detachments for their protection. But the passes of the
Asturian mountains were blocked up by snow,
and Romana was consequently obliged, on the
approach of Soult, to push across the Astorga.

The consequence was, that all the houses in Astorga were filled with Spanish soldiers, and the roads were literally obstructed with men, horses, cars, and all the other accompaniments of an army which had foundered or broken down on the march. It is scarcely possible to conceive anything more wretched than the condition of Romana's army. They wanted clothing, accoutrements, arms, ammunition. and even food. A malignant fever had broken out among them, and the number of the sick was hourly augmenting. Never did any congregation of human beings exhibit less external semblance of a military body.. The soldiers under arms little exceeded in number the sick borne on cars and mules ; and, as they passed slowly along, enfeebled and emaciated by disease, the procession had more the appearance of an ambulatory hospital, than of a force by which the country was to be defended. Such was the condition of the army of Romana. Let it also be recorded, that this brave and suffering band bore their multiplied privations with unshrinking patience ; that they uniformly displayed, even in the very depth of their misfortunes, a courage and devotion worthy of that cause, in behalf of which they were alike prepared to bleed, or suffer. Before his arrival at Astorga, Sir John Moore, notwithstanding his assurances to Romana, had resigned all thoughts of making a stand in the neighborhood of that city. From the prisoners taken on the preceeding day, it was ascertained that the head-quarters of Napoleon's army, had on the preceding evening, been at Villalpando, a village only sixteen miles distant. No defensive preparations had been attempted, and the General determined to continue the retreat on Villa Franca. Of this measure Romana disapproved. He declared himself ready to join the English army in defending the strong ground around Astorga, from whence a secure retreat would, in any event, be open to them, by the almost impregnable passes of Manzanal and Foncebadon, which a small body might successfully maintain against any numbers. This project, however, did not meet the approbation of Sir John Moore. Instant preparations were made for retreat. The stores, of which Astorga had been made the depot, were destroyed or distributed among the Spanish troops, and the sick were abandoned to the enemy. In the miserable condition of the Spanish army, it might have been supposed, that this half-naked, half-armed, half-famished, and diseased multitude would have sought protection in their retreat from the English columns. It was not so. With a spirit which death alone could extinguish, this suffering, but high-minded band, still confided in their own exertions to keep the field; and when Sir John Moore proposed to Romana that he should retire by

Orense, the proposal was instantly acceded to.
Romana only requested that the British troops
might be restrained from the further perpetration
of those acts of disgraceful violence which had
hitherto marked their progress: a request which
must have imbittered the spirit of Sir John Moore,
to know that his power was inadequate to grant.
At Astorga the light brigades under Gen. Crawford separated from the army and marched by
way of Orense to Vigo, where Sir John Moore had
directed transports to be sent for the embarkation
of the army. This detachment preceded Romana's
army in the line of march, and when the miserable band of patriots, after a halt of only one night,
took their way to Orense, they found the country
through which they passed, already stripped of
supplies. This completed the wreck of this gallant but unfortunate army. The infantry became
at length completely disorganized, and Romana
with the cavalry and guns, retired to the valley of
the Mincio. On the 1st of January, 1809, Napoleon entered Astorga and formed a junction with
Marshall Soult. Leaving Ney with eighteen thous-
and men to keep Leon in subjection, he directed
Soult by forced marches to continue the pursuit.
This was done with uncommon vigor. On the
night of the 1st, so closely did they already press
on our rear, that their patroles fell in with the
piquets of our rear-guard. In the meanwhile

Napoleon countermarched with the rest of his army, and in a few days returned to France. It is melancholy to contemplate the condition to which we had already been reduced. During the march to Villa Franca, the rain came down in torrents; men and horses, sinking through fatigue, covered the roads, and the soldiers whose strength still enabled them to proceed, maddened by the continued suffering of cold and hunger, were no longer under any subordination. In such circumstances, pillage could not be prevented. Wherever we came the inhabitants fled from their dwellings and sought shelter among the mountains. Enormities of all kinds were committed, houses and even villages were burning in all directions. The ravages of the most ferocious enemy could not have exceeded in atrocity those perpetrated by a British army on their allies. At Benevente an order had heen issued by the General assuring the army that the only object of the retiring movement was, not to evacuate the country, but to secure a more favorable position. It had, therefore, been confidently expected, that a stand would be made at the almost impregnable defiles through which the army passed after quitting Villa Franca. The country had been traversed by Sir David Baird on his advance; and it was generally held incredible, that the retreat should be continued beyond that point. The sufferings which the army had already endur-

ed, and the lamentable want of discipline, to which
the rapidity of the retreat had given rise, tended
to strengthen the conviction that the General would
gladly avail himself of the great defensive advantages which the country afforded him.   This hope
was disappointed.   Sir John Moore saw no safety
but in embarkation ; and the retreat was continued with unrelenting speed.   At every step of their
progress however, the misfortunes of our devoted
army seemed to accumulate.   The mortality among
the horses was excessive, and no sooner did these
noble animals become unable to proceed, than
they were shot, in order to prevent their being serviceable to the enemy.   The ammunition wagons,
which had hitherto kept up, were falling one by
one to the rear, and the ammunition they contained was destroyed.   In the towns, many of the soldiers, in the recklessness of despair, broke into the
cellars, and giving way to the most desperate excess, were found dead by the enemy.   During the
marches the number of stragglers was enormous.
Under different pretexts, whole regiments strayed
from their colors ; and, as often as a store or wine
house was discovered, scenes of the most revolting
character insued.   The enemy's cavalry was con-
tinually pressing on our rear, and, under such circumstances, no pause could be made to afford protection, to those, who, from intoxication or exhaustion of strength were compelled to fall behind.   I

might here mention an incident which occurred near Benevente. While we were halting at a Convent, in order to refresh and cover the retreat of the army, the bugle sounded the alarm and we hastily commenced our march. A soldier of our company left his wife stupid with intoxication in the third story of the Convent. Hardly had we evacuated the place, when it was occupied by the enemy, and the woman, by some of the soldiers, was thrown from the window and most horribly mangled. At Bembibre in particular, the town on the departure of the reserve was filled with these unfortunate wretches. Every effort was made to save them from the miserable fate which they so madly courted; but in vain. The rear-guard was at length compelled to march. A small detachment of cavalry still remained, in hopes that some at least of the victims might be rescued. But the enemy came on in force, and the French dragoons, charging onward, through a crowd of men, women and children, slashed to the right and left with their sabres, sparing neither age nor sex. Never did I gaze on a spectacle more appalling than those who, escaping death, came up bleeding and lacerated, and were, by order of the General, paraded through the ranks, as a warning to their comrades. It is well that these humiliating circumstances should be recorded. It is well that war should be gazed on in all its aspects, and not unprofitable perhaps, that such episodes should be commemorated in the emblazoned volume of our victories. Since the affair of the 28th December, no engagement had taken place. On the 3d of January, the advanced guard of the enemy were seen advancing on Cacabelos. The town is divided by a rivulet, along the banks of which, part of the reserve was stationed. On a hill about half a league in front, were posted the 95th Rifle corps, and the piquet of cavalry. The General ordered the 95th to retire through the town by a bridge. While this order was executing, the French cavalry came on in force, driving the piquet before them, and charging the rear companies, which had not yet crossed the bridge, succeeded in making some prisoners. The enemy supposing they had thrown our rear-guard into confusion, immediately advanced a body of dismounted chasseurs, who, dashing forward through the stream with great spirit, attacked the 95th, who had barely gained time to extend in skirmishing order. The regiment received the attack with admirable steadiness, and retreating up a hill, in rear of the town, took post among some vineyards, from which they continued to gall the enemy by a well-directed fire. From this position the French cavalry attempted to dislodge them, but without success. The 95th again repulsed them ; and they retreated with the loss of a considerable number in killed and wounded. General Colbert, an officer of great gallantry and distinction, was among the number of the former. In a short time after, a strong body of the enemy's infantry was observed on the opposite hills, in full march on our position. The artillery was instantly ordered to open its fire, which it did with such precision as to check the advance of the French column, which retired with considerable loss, and without firing a shot. From Villa Franca, the country afforded no field for the action of cavalry ; and it was therefore ordered to precede the infantry by forced marches to Lugo, where the leading division was directed to concentrate. Towards this point, also, the infantry were pushed on with increased speed, and, if possible, with augmented suffering. The road was bestrewed by the bodies of men dead and dying. But the agonies of women were still more dreadful to behold. Of these, by some strange neglect, or by some mistaken sentiment of humanity, an unusually large proportion had been suffered to accompany the army. Some of these unhappy creatures were taken in labor on the road, and amid the storms of sleet and snow, gave birth to infants, which, with their mothers, perished as soon as they had seen the light. The wife of Sergeant Thomas, my pay Sergeant, of Capt. Dalziel's company, was among the unfortunate sufferers. Others, in the unconquerable energy of maternal love,

would toil on with one or two children on their
backs; till on looking round, they perceived that
the hapless objects of their attachment were frozen
to death. But more frightful even than this, was the
depth of moral degradation to which these wretched followers of the camp were frequently reduced.
Nothing could be more appalling to the heart, than
to hear the dreadful curses and imprecations which
burst from the livid lips of intoxicated and de-
spairing women, as they laid them down to die.
I am well aware that the horrors of this retreat
have been, again and again, described in terms
calculated to freeze the blood of such as read them;
but I have no hesitation in saying, that the most
harrowing accounts which have yet been laid before the public, fall short of the reality. The distance between Villa Franca and Lugo was accomplished by the reserve in forty-eight hours.
During this march, a quantity of valuable stores
was distroyed; but the necessity of repose, to re-
cruit the exhausted soldiers, became at length ap-
parent to Sir John Moore. At Lugo the army
halted on the 6th, and the General took up a position in front of the town, with the intention of offering battle to the enemy. Never did any measure produce a more striking and instantaneous
revulsion of feeling in the troops. Insubordination
was at an end, stragglers hastened to join their
regiments, worn frames became reanimated with

vigor, and the promiscuous assemblage of disor-
derly soldiers became again invested with all the
attributes of a disciplined army. It was at length
ascertained by the General, that Corunna was a
more eligible place for embarkation than Vigo;
and as it besides possessed the advantage of being
considerably nearer, it was determined to direct
the march of the army to that point. Orders therefore had been dispatched to recall the light-bri-
gades and the division of Gen. Frazer, which had
been previously directed to proceed to Vigo. These
orders were transmitted to Sir David Baird by a
staff-officer, but the orderly-dragoon who was employed by Sir David Baird to convey the despatch
to its destination, unfortunately got drunk, and
lost it. This occurrence was productive of the
worst effects. Gen. Frazer's troops had proceeded a full day on their march, before the order
reached them; and, in consequence, without food
or rest, were compelled to retrace their steps, and
arrived at Lugo with the loss of four hundred of
their number. The ground on which Sir John
Moore proposed to receive the enemy's attack at
Lugo, was selected with skill. The right of the
position rested on the Tamboga, its front extended along the sides of a strong ravine; and the left,
somewhat withdrawn was protected by precipitous acclivities. About mid-day on the 6th, the
French columns were observed to be advancing

on the English position.   Preparation was immediately made for their reception ; but no engagement ensued.   The French took possession of a
strong mountainous ridge in front of the British ;
and formed in order of battle seemed to challenge
attack.   For several hours did the lines thus continue gazing on each other, without hostile movement on either side.   The hope of battle gradually faded ; at last evening closed, and the troops
returned to their quarters. On the following morning the enemy advanced four guns protected by a
few squadrons of cavalry, towards the centre, and
commenced a sharp cannonade.   The fire was immediately returned by us, with such effect that
one of their guns was dismounted, and the rest
silenced.   For above an hour, no farther hostili-
ties took place.   The enemy then made a feint on
our   right   in   order   to   cover   the   advance of
five guns and a strong column of infantry on our
left.   Sir John Moore immediately rode at full
speed to that part of our line.   In the meanwhile
a warm skirmish had taken place with the piquets,
which were driven hastily back.   The enemy's
column were already ascending the height occu-
ed by the 76th regiment, which gradually fell back,
until joined by the 51st, when, after a few dis-
charges of musketry, these regiments advanced to
the charge and drove back the French in confusion.   The setting in of night again disappointed

the hope of immediate engagement; and our army retired to their quarters with the fervent wish that the dawn of morning might light them to battle. Sir John Moore was impressed with the conviction that this wish would be realized. He considered the preceding attack as made only, by Marshall Soult, with the view of reconnoitering the strength of the force opposed to him, and expected that the day following would produce a more general engagement. In this he was disappointed. On the morning of the 8th, the French were still observed in their position, yet hour after hour passed, and they made no movement. At length night fell, and with it fell all the fond hopes which had been cherished by the army. In order to deceive the enemy, large fires were lighted along the line; and at ten o'clock our army again commenced their retreat. No sooner did Marshall Soult become aware of the evasion of his enemy, than the pursuit was immediately recommenced, and followed up with unabated vigor; but we had already gained so much ground, that it was not till evening that the enemy's advanced guard came up with our rear.

The horrors of this march were of the most aggravated description. The night was dark and stormy, the cold intense and the sleet fell heavily. The troops already jaded and half-famished, and many of them barefoot, marched along roads knee-deep in mud. Insubordination again spread among the ranks and the number of stragglers was enormous. About ten in the morning the army arrived at Valmeda. Here positive exhaustion compelled a halt, and the men lay on the open ground for several hours, exposed to the continual action of a heavy rain. But even this brief interval was not granted to undisturbed repose. A cry arose from time to time, that the enemy were advancing; and, at each alarm, the troops were ordered to fall in. Such an intermission was little calculated to refresh the worn strength of the soldiers, and, towards evening, when they again resumed their march, little benefit was found to have resulted from the halt.

In the north of Spain, every village has a common oven for baking, where the whole village bake their bread on a fixed day. About dark we arrived at a village where, it being the day for baking, the bread had just been put into the oven. The quarter-master of each regiment was ordered to remain until the bread was baked, which was then to be distributed to each regiment. Whilst the quarter-masters and head-baker were watching the oven, the soldiers took the advantage of removing the bread by making a breach with their bayonets upon the outside of the oven. I got about a pound of bread and it was to me a welcome morsel, though it was not quite baked.

On the 10th, the army halted at Betanzos; and Gen. Paget, with the reserve, remained in position a few miles in front of that town, for the protection of the stragglers. The conduct of this officer, and the troops he commanded throughout the retreat was such as to command the admiration of the army. The reserve marched better and bore their sufferings with greater resolution than any other portion of the troops; and the skill, promptitude and unwearied vigilance of Gen. Paget, were, on every occasion remarkable. From Betanzos the army accomplished its march to Corunna, with little molestation from the enemy. A bridge near the town was attempted to be destroyed, but without success. At Astorga, the General had ordered the whole of the engineer's equipments to be burned; and the army were thus most imprudently deprived of the power of impeding the progress of the enemy, which the destruction of the numerous bridges, would have afforded. Near Corunna however, the bridge across the Mero was blown up, the necessary tools for the purpose having been brought from the town; but owing to the premature explosion of a mine, the superintending officer of engineers was killed. The army had now reached their destined point of embarkation, but the transports had not yet arrived from Vigo. Only a few ships lay in the harbor, on board of which the sick who preceded the army were im-

mediately embarked, and it became necessary that
the army should assume a position, and once more
show front to the enemy.   That this necessity was
imposed on Sir John Moore. never to any Fnglish-
man can be a matter of regret.   It saved the British army from the disgrace of having quitted Spain
like downcast and disheartened fugitives, of having sought refuge in their ships from the hostility
of an enemy, with whom they had never measur-
ed strength in combat.

Sir John Moore preceded the army on its march
to Corunna, and surveyed the country in its neighborhood.   There were two ranges of heights in
front of the town.   The higher and more distant
of these would, unquestionably, have afforded
a position of considerable strength, had the numerical force of the army been sufficient for its occupation.   But, as this was not the case, it became
necessary to occupy the nearer range, though of
inferior altitude.   Such, however, were the dis-
advantages of this position, that some of the general officers recommended Sir John Moore to pro-
pose terms to Soult, in order to induce him to per-
mit the army to embark unmolested.   Sir John
Moore, however, declared himself averse from
adopting this melancholy and disgraceful altera-
tive, and besides was exceedingly doubtful, whether any such proposal, if made, would be attended with success.   Most fortunately, therefore, for

his own fame and for the honor of the army he
commanded, this degrading counsel was rejected,
and England was not destined to blush for her
sons. The enemy were now rapidly collecting on
the Mero, and it became necessary that arrangements should be promptly made for the impending
battle. The division of General Hope, to which
I belonged, was directed to occupy a ridge on the
left, commanding the road to Betanzos, and slop-
ing with a gradual declivity towards Elvina. The
post of Sir David Baird's division was on the right,
extending from Elvina along the series of heights,
which bent in an oblique direction towards the
front, and terminated in a valley which divided
this range from another on the opposite side of the
Vigo road. The rifle-corps was ordered to form
a chain across the valley. The reserve under
General Paget was posted at Airis, a small village
in the rear of the centre. The left flank of this
position was well protected by the high banks of
the Mero, but the right was weak; it rested on
the village of Elvina, situated low down, at the
extremity of the hills on which the front of the
army was formed. To remedy this defect, the division of General Frazer was posted about half a
mile in rear of the right, on some high ground commanding the road to Vigo. The artillery was disposed along the front of the line. During the whole
of the 13th, Sir John Moore was occupied in ma-

king these dispositions.   Having completed them,
he returned to his quarters, and, writing his last
dispatch, directed Brig. Gen. Stewart to proceed
with it to England.

On the 14th January, the enemy commenced a
cannonade on the left, which was returned by our
artillery, with such effect, that the French at last
drew off their guns.   In the evening the transports
from Vigo hove in sight.   On the heights, about a
league distant from the town, was a powder magazine, which it was deemed advisable to destroy.
It contained about four thousand barrels of gunpowder, which had been brought from England
some months before, and by an unpardonable negligence, had been suffered to remain in store,
while the Spanish armies were without ammunition.   A few hundred barrels had, on the preceding day been removd to Corunna, the remainder
was directed to be blown up.   The explosion was
tremendous.   Corunna shook, as if convulsed by
an earthquake.   Huge masses of rock were cast
from their pedestals.   The calm waters in the bay
became furiously agitated.   A vast column of
smoke and dust arose perpendicularly and slowly
to a great height, and then bursting with a roar-
ing sound, a shower of stones and fragments of all
kinds reverted to the earth, killing several persons
who had incautiously remained too near the scene
of peril.   A stillness, only interrupted by the lash-

ing of the waves on the shore, succeeded, and the business of war went on.

On the arrival of the transports, preparations were immediately made for the embarkation of the army. With the exception of eight British and four Spanish guns, the artillery was sent on board, the ground being considered unfavorable for its use. The dismounted cavalry and a few horses were likewise embarked,—the remainder were shot.

The bridge of El Burgo, having been repaired, two divisions of infantry, and one of cavalry passed the Mero, and, driving back our outposts, marched into position. On the 15th, Delaborde's division followed, and took post on the height of Portoso, forming the right of the army. The ground thus chosen by the enemy, was the ridge of rocky and irregular heights by which our position was nearly encompassed. Their right was placed on the Betanzos and St. Jago roads, and their left rested on a hill covered with wood, overlooking our line, of which, after some resistance from the light troops, they succeeded in gaining possession. In the evening, Col. Mackenzie of the 5th perceived two of the enemy's guns not far distant, and imagined that by a sudden attack he might surprise them. The attempt failed. Col. Mackenzie was killed during the advance, and his party were driven back with loss. During the night of the

15th, Marshall Soult-succeeded in establishing a battery of eleven guns on the wooded hill, at the extremity of his left. This was an operation of great difficulty. The ground was rúgged; the French were in possession of no road, and the horses were weak and exhausted. By great exertion however, the object was accomplished; and the French thus acquired a decided superiority in point of artillery.

BATTLE OF CORUNNA.

The preparations for embarking were completed on the morning of the 16th, and Sir John Moore gave notice, that, in case the enemy should not move during the day, the embarkation of the reserve should commence at four o'clock. The tranquility of the armies remained undisturbed till noon, when the General mounted his horse and rode off to visit the outposts. He had not proceeded far when he received a report from Gen. Hope, stating that the enemy's line were getting under arms; and a deserter who came in at the same moment, confirmed the intelligence. He spurred forward. The piquets had already opened fire on the enemy's light troops, which were pouring rapidly down on the right wing A heavy fire was shortly opened from the French battery on the height; the piquets were driven rapidly back; and four strong columns of the enemy, supported by a reserve, were observed descending the hill.

Two of these, one emerging from the wood, the other skirting its edge, threatened the right of the position; another directed its march on the centre; and the fourth on the left.

The two first of these columns advanced with rapidity, and by a bold attack at once carried the village of Elvina. Thus far successful, they endeavored to turn the right of the position. It was defended by Lord Wm. Bentinck's brigade, having the brigade of Guards in their rear. In order to prevent the success of this manœuvre, Gen. Paget was ordered to advance with the reserve, and take post on the right of the line. Lord William Bentinck's brigade received the attack with firmness and the fourth regiment being thrown back *en potence*, met the enemy with a well directed fire. The order was at length given to charge; and the 42d and 50th regiments advanced to regain the village of Elvina. The ground around the village was so intersected by walls and enclosures, as to prevent any general collision.

A severe but irregular fight ensued, which terminated in the French being driven back with great loss. The 50th regiment led by Major Napier, rushed into Elvina, and with great gallantry drove out the enemy with the bayonet, and pursued him for some distance beyond it. In the meanwhile, from some misapprehension the 42d had retired, and the enemy being reinforced took

advantage of that circumstance to renew the conflict. Elvina became again the scene of struggle;
the 42d after a brief but animating address from
the General, returned to the attack, and the Guards
being brought up to their support, the enemy gave
way. It was at this period of the action that Sir
John Moore received his death wound. He was
engaged in watching the result of the contest about
Elvina, when a cannon shot struck him on the
breast and beat him to the ground. He raised
himself immediately to a sitting posture, and continued with a calm gaze to regard the regiments engaged in front. Captain Hardinge threw himself
from his horse, and took him by the hand; then
observing his anxiety, he told him the 42d were advancing, and on this intelligence, his countenance
was observed to brighten. His friend, Col. Graham now dismounted, and from the composure
of his features entertained hopes that he was not
even wounded, but observing the horrid laceration
and effusion of blood, he rode off for surgical assistance. Sir John Moore was removed from the
field by a party of the 42d. As the soldiers placed
him in a blanket, his sword became entangled,
and the hilt entered the wound. Capt. Hardinge
attempted to take it off, but he stopped him, saying, " it is as well as it is, I had rather it should go
out of the field with me." Sir David Baird had
previously been disabled by a severe wound; and

the command of the army now devolved on Gen.
Hope. In the meanwhile, all went prosperously
in the field. The reserve pushed on to the right,
and driving back the enemy, continued advancing
on their flank, overthrowing every thing before
them. The enemy perceiving their left wing to
be exposed, drew it entirely back. An attack
made on our centre, was successfully resisted by
the brigades of Generals Manningham and Leith.
The ground in that quarter being more elevated
and favorable for artillery, the guns were of great
service. On the left, the enemy had taken possession of the village of Palario on the road to Betanzos. From this a fire was still kept up by their
troops, till Col. Nichols, at the head of some companies of the 14th attacked it and beat them out.
Day was now fast closing, and the enemy had
lost ground in all parts of the field. The firing
however still continued, and night alone brought
the contest to a close. Thus ended the battle of
Corunna, a glorious termination to an inglorious
retreat.

While Sir John Moore was removing from the
field, the expression of his countenance remained
unchanged, and he gave utterance to no expression
of pain. From this circumstance, Capt. Hardinge
gathered temporary hope, that the wound might
not be mortal, and expressed it to the dying General. Hearing this, he turned his head for a moment, and looking steadfastly at the wound, said,

"*No, Hardinge, I feel that to be impossible.*" Several times he caused his attendants to stop and turn him round, that he might gaze on the field of battle, and when the firing indicated the advance of the British, he signified his satisfaction and permitted the bearers to proceed. On examination by the surgeons, the wound of Sir John Moore was at once pronounced to be mortal, and from increasing pain, he could speak but with difficulty. Observing his friend Colonel Anderson by his bed, he asked if the French were beaten, and then said, "*You know, Anderson I have always wished to die this way—you will see my friends as soon as you can. Tell them everything. Say to my mother—*" Here his voice failed from agitation, and he did not again venture to name her. When his strength was fast waning, and little more than a glimmering of life remained, he said to Col. Anderson, "*I hope the people of England will be satisfied, I hope my country will do me justice.*" After a while, he pressed the hand of Col. Anderson to his body ; and in a few minutes died without a struggle. Thus fell Sir John Moore. Kind in feeling, generous in spirit, dauntless in heart,—no man was more beloved ; none more lamented.

The night succeeding the action was passed in the embarkation of the troops. At ten o'clock they moved off the field by brigades and marched down to Corunna. Major General Beresford was posted with the rear-guard, on the lines fronting

Corunna, to watch the motions of the enemy. Major Gen. Hill, with his brigade, was stationed on an eminence behind the town, ready to afford support to Beresford, if necessary. The embarktion proceeded rapidly during the night, and no attempt was made to molest the covering brigades. On the following morning however, the enemy pushed forward a body of light troops to the heights of St. Lucia, which commanded the harbor, and, planting a few cannon, fired at the transports. At three o'clock Gen. Hill's brigade was withdrawn, and at night the rear-guard embarked without molestation from the enemy.

At twelve o'clock on the night of the 16th, the remains of Sir John Moore were removed to the citadel of Corunna. He had often said, that, if killed in battle, he wished to be buried where he fell; and it was determined that the body should be interred on the rampart of the citadel. A grave was dug by a party of the 9th regiment, the aides-de-camp attending by turns. No coffin could be procured; and the body without being undressed, was wrapt by the officers of his staff in a military cloak and blankets. The interment was hastened, for, about eight in the morning the sound of firing was heard, and they feared that, in the event of a serious attack, they might be prevented from paying their last duties to their General. The officers of his family bore him to the grave; the funeral service was read by the Chaplain; and the corpse was covered with earth.   The following is a beautiful and touching description of his burial, written by the Rev. Charles Wolfe, a graduate of the University of Dublin.

THE BURIAL OF SIR JOHN MOORE.

" Not a drum was heard, not a funeral note,
As his corse to the rampart we hurried.
Not a soldier discharged his farewell shot,
O'er the grave where our hero we buried.

We buried him darkly, at dead of night,
The sods with our bayonets turning;
By the struggling moonbeam's misty light,
And the lantern dimly burning.

No useless coffin enclosed his breast,
Not in sheet or in shroud we wound him;
But he lay like a warrior taking his rest,
With his martial cloak around him.

Few and short were the prayers we said,
And we spoke not a word of sorrow;
But we steadfastly gazed on the face that was dead,
And we bitterly thought of the morrow.

We thought, as we hollowed his narrow bed,
And smoothed down his lonely pillow,
That the foe, and the stranger would tread o'er his head,
And we far away on the billow!

Lightly they'll talk of the spirit that's gone,
And o'er his cold ashes upbraid him,—
But little he'll reck, if they let him sleep on
In the grave where a Briton has laid him.

But half of our heavy task was done,
When the clock struck the hour for retiring;
And we heard the distant and random gun
Of the enemy suddenly firing.

Slowly and sadly we laid him down,
From the field of his fame fresh and gory,
We carved not a line and we raised not a stone—
But we left him alone with his glory!

During the retreat to Corunna, his country sustained a severe loss in the death of Major General Anstruther. No man had more honorably distintinguished himself by zeal, gallantry and talent. He died of inflammation of the lungs, brought on by exposure to the extreme inclemency of the weather. His devotion to the service induced him to neglect the precautions and remedies his situation required; and he continued to perform his duty till approaching dissolution rendered farther exertion impossible. When no longer able to mount his horse, he was placed in a carriage and conveyed to Corunna. There he expired amid the universal regret of his fellow soldiers; and his remains were deposited in a grave on the ramparts, near that of his commander.

On the 22d April, 1809, Sir Arthur Wellesley returned to Lisbon, and was invested with the supreme command in Portugal. From the period of that event, a new era commenced in the war. His appointment gave unity of action and purpose to the British and Portuguese forces, and at once put a stop to those unfortunate jealousies and distractions, which had already occurred but too frequently between the leaders of the allied armies. The French were gradually adding to their conquests, nothing but the prompt and decisive measures which Wellesley now commenced taking, could have turned the unpromising aspect of affairs. His first step was directed against Soult, in order,

if possible, to drive him at once out of Portugal,
before he could effect a union with Victor, upon
whom, now at the head of thirty thousand men, he
meditated a subsequent attack. Quitting Lisbon
towards the end of April, Sir Arthur arrived at
Coimbra, on the 5th of May, and a few days after
set out for Oporto. In the meanwhile, the object
of these movements could not be supposed to escape the penetration of Soult. He saw the danger
of being speedily enclosed in the north of Portugal, and determined to extricate himself from the
increasing perils of his position, by evacuating the
country. Measures were accordingly adopted for
this purpose. Preparations were instantly set on
foot for removing the sick and the baggage ; and
having destroyed the pontoon-bridge across the
Douro, and given orders that all the boats should
be brought to the right bank of the river, he imagined himself secure from immediate attack. He
imagined too that Sir Arthur Wellesley would
avail himself of his maritime resources, and embarking his troops, endeavor to effect a landing
near the mouth of the Douro. This would have
allowed time for the leisurely retreat of the army ;
and orders were despatched to Loison requiring
him to maintain his ground at Mezamfrio and Pe-
za da Ragoa, in order to prevent the passage of
the river being effected at either of these points.
Had the calculations of Soult been realized, with
regard to his enemy's intentions, no obstruction

would have existed to his retreat into Gallicia ; or by advancing on Beresford with his whole force, he might have crossed into Beira. But Sir Arthur Wellesley had bolder measures in contemplation. He determined at once to cross the river, and drive the enemy from Oporto.

PASSAGE OF THE DOURO.

With this view, General Murray was detached to Avintas, a ford about five miles higher up, where he was directed to cross the river with his brigade, and send down any boats which he might be able to procure. The brigade of Guards, under General Sherbrooke, received orders to cross the ferry below the city at Villa Nuova. The main body under his own immediate command, were to attempt a passage at the Convent of St. Augustino da Serra, which occupies a height nearly opposite to the town. The Douro was at that spot nearly three hundred yards broad, extremely rapid, with considerable heights on the right bank, and a large unfinished building designed for the Bishop's palace, which could be made serviceable as a post of defence by those who first landed, till sufficient numbers should have crossed the river, to enable them to advance on the town. To protect the passage, several guns had been planted in the garden of the convent. By aid of the inhabitants, two boats had been procured from the opposite side of the river, and in these, three companies of the

Buffs, immediately passed the river. Other boats were speedily despatched by the zeal of the people; and the embarkation of the troops was rapidly continued. General Paget was among the first detachment; he immediately took possession of the unfinished building already mentioned, and defended it with great gallantry, till the arrival of the 48th, and 60th, and a Portuguese battalion, when the contest was continued on more equal terms. Early in the engagement, General Paget lost an arm, and the command devolved on Gen. Hill, who was still warmly contesting the ground, when the brigade of Guards and the 29th regiment appeared on the enemy's right; and in the opposite direction the troops were seen approaching from Avintas. Under these circumstances the enemy's column fell back in confusion. We charged up the streets of Oporto, making many prisoners, amid the most animated demonstrations of joyful welcome from the inhabitants. Handkerchiefs were waved to us from balconies and windows, blessings were breathed on the brave deliverers of the city, mingled, on all hands, with shouts of joyful and triumphant greeting. Confusion and disorder had spread through the whole French army. The panic seemed even to increase when they gained the open country; and Major Harvey with a single squadron of the 14th dragoons, charged through three battalions of French infantry, marching in a hollow road, and brought off many prisoners, without sustaining any considerable loss. Unfortunately, however, it was found impossible to take full advantage of the panic of the enemy, by continuing the pursuit. The army were without supplies of any kind; the rapidity of the advance from Coimbra, having outstripped the most active exertions of the commissariat. The fatigue the troops had undergone rendered repose necessary; and the pursuit was, therefore, relinquished at the approach of the evening. Had these obstacles not intervened, there can be little doubt that the whole army of Marshall Soult would have been destroyed.

As it was however, nothing could exceed the boldness and the brilliance of the operations of Sir Arthur Wellesley. The Douro had been passed in open day, in the very face of a powerful enemy. One of the ablest and most experienced of the French marshalls, had been taken by surprise, and his army driven from Oporto, with the loss of its sick and wounded, of a great part of its baggage and of a considerable number of guns. Our head-quarters were established in the very house which Marshall Soult had occupied, and a dinner in preparation for him was served up at the table of Sir Arthur. The loss of our army, amounted to only twenty-three men killed and ninety-eight wounded.

On the following day we made arrangements for pursuing the enemy, but gave up the pursuit at

Montalegre, whilst Soult crossed the frontier at
Alhariz and retreated to Orense.

Sir Arthur now prepared for operations against
Victor, and about the middle of June, arrived at
Abrantes, whence after being detained some days
by a want of supplies, and by the sickness of his
troops, he commenced his march into Spain at the
end of the month; and on the 12th of July he
reached Placentia, where a conference took place
with Cuesta, the Spanish General, by which it was
agreed, that the British and Spanish armies should
proceed to attack Victor on the eighteenth. No
action however occurred until the 27th. In the
meanwhile, Joseph accompanied by Marshall Jourdan, with all their disposable troops, had effected
an union with Victor. Immediate orders were
despatched to Soult to form a junction with Ney
and Mortier, and advance on Placentia, with the
view of intercepting the line of operations of the
allied armies and cutting off their retreat.

The situation of Sir Arthur had now become
critical in the extreme. The army in his front
amounted to about fifty thousand men ; that advancing in his rear was considerably stronger. In
such circumstances had the army under Joseph remained on the defensive,—as it was their obvious
policy to have done,—no choice remained to the
British General, but to attack them under all advantages of position, or to retreat. In the former

case he could have derived little support from the Spanish army, whose want of steadiness and discipline disqualified them from manœuvring in presence of an enemy enjoying all the advantages of ground. In the latter case, the only road open was to the southward of the Tagus ; and, to effect the passage of that river, when closely followed by a powerful enemy, would necessarily have been an operation of great difficulty and danger. Such was the situation of Sir Arthur Wellesley before the battle of Talavera. From much of its danger. he was fortunately extricated by the blunder of the enemy, who determined on attacking the allied armies in their position.

BATTLE OF TALAVERA.

The ground occupied by the allies was about two miles in extent. The Spanish army was on the right, the British on the left of the line.ʹ The position of the former was extremely strong, being almost unapproachable, from the mud enclosures of olive grounds, and vineyards in their front, and they were so posted in the ravines which abounded, as to be sheltered from the enemy's artillery. Their right was *appuyed* by the Tagus ; their left by the British. The ground on the centre and left of the line was more open, but intersected with roads leading to the town ; and the front of the whole position was covered by a ravine formed by the winter torrents, but then dry. The left

flank of the British rested on an eminence of considerable boldness, and their right on another
somewhat lower, on which a redoubt had been begun, in order to secure the connection of the armies, but was not sufficiently advanced to add
much to the security of the troops stationed for defence of the height. These consisted of two brigades of infantry, under Brig. Gen. Campbell, supported by a battery of about ten guns, The Guards,
General Cameron's brigade, and the German legion, formed the centre, under Lieut. Gen. Sherbrooke. The division of General Hill was on the
left where two brigades of artillery were posted for
defence of the hill in which the position terminated. The remainder of the guns were distributed
on the most favorable points along the line. The
cavalry was commanded by Lieut. Gen. Payne.
Major General Cotton's light brigade, to which I,
on this day, belonged, supported the right and centre. Brig. Gen. Anson's and the heavy brigade
under Gen. Fane were on the left. The Spanish
infantry was formed in two lines, and in rear of
the left the Duke del Albuquerque was stationed
with the main body of the Spanish cavalry. Subsequently a detachment of about three thousand
light-infantry under Don Louis Bassecourt, was
moved to the valley below the British left, in order
to observe the movements of a body of the enemy which appeared in the mountains beyond, but·

at too great a distance to exert any influence on the contest. A division of infantry, and a brigade of cavalry under Gen. Mackenzie had been stationed in the wood on the right of the Alberche, which covered the left of the British army. About noon this advanced force was suddenly attacked by the enemy, who succeeded in penetrating between the two brigades of which it was composed. Some confusion ensued, but order was speedily restored by the exertions of the officers, and the retreat was finely covered by the brigade of Col. Donkin which retired and took up its position with perfect regularity and steadiness. The division of Gen. Mackenzie was then posted as a second line in rear of the centre. In this affair, Sir Arthur Wellesley narrowly escaped being made prisoner. He had ascended a tower immediately in rear of Mackenzie's division, to observe the motions of the enemy. Fortunately he observed the troops to falter, and descended barely in time to escape by throwing himself on his horse in the midst of the affray. In the meantime the enemy continued to push on his columns, and a partial action ensued along the whole front of the line. A division of cavalry advanced towards the right of the allies, and threatened the town of Talavera. But the difficulties of the ground and the fire of the Spanish batteries, soon obliged them to retreat. A body of about five thousand Spaniards, however, though posted in the strongest manner threw down their arms and fled. So indignat was Cuesta at this dastardly conduct, that, after the action he ordered the division to be decimated; and it was only at the earnest entreaty of Sir Arthur Wellesly,-that he consented to a second decimation of those on whom the lot had fallen. In consequence only six officers, and about thirty men were executed.

Under these circumstances, the whole French army, in number about about fifty thousand, assembled in front of the position occupied by the allies. Towards evening, a resolute attempt was made to gain possession of a hill on the left, which was regarded as the key of the position. The enemy advanced at double-quick time to the assault, covered by a heavy cannonade. The attack being unexpected, was for a moment successful, and the French gained possession of the height; but the 48th and 29th regiments, being brought up by General Hill, poured in a volley; and the 29th by a most splendid charge, drove back the enemy in confusion, and established themselves on the summit. In the course of the night another attempt was made to carry this important post. This too was unfortunate. Col. Donkin's brigade had been moved up to support the troops on the hill; and the enemy were repulsed with little difficulty. The loss on both sides during this attack was considerable. Gen. Hill was at one time surrounded by the enemy, and received a wound in the shoulder.

The troops lay all night upon their arms in expectation of attack. At two in the morning the Spanish line was alarmed by the approach of the enemy's light-troops, who were received by a brisk charge of musketry, which ceased in about ten minutes, and the silence of night again prevailed on the field of battle. At length day broke on the contending armies, drawn up in battle array, in the positions which they respectively occupied at the commencement of the action on the preceding evening. At five o'clock, two strong columns of the French were formed in front of the height, which they had already twice vainly attempted to carry. Under cover of a tremendous fire from fifty pieces of cannon, the columns advanced across a ravine which ran along the front of the position, and ascended the acclivity on which were posted the brigades of Gen. Tilson and Gen. Richard Stewart. By the troops under these officers they were received with the utmost gallantry and steadiness. A heavy fire of musquetry on both sides was followed by a charge from the British; and the assailants were driven back at the bayonet's point with great slaughter. The British cavalry were ordered up to charge the right flank of the retiring column, but unfortunately it was at too great a distance. The object, however, was too important to be lightly given up by the enemy. The attempt on the height was repeatedly made, and repeatedly terminated in a similar result, till, dis-

heartened by the uniform failure of their efforts,
they retired from the scene of contest, leaving the
ground covered with their dead. About eleven
o'clock the firing ceased. A period of truce was
tacitly recognised by both armies, which the
French employed in cooking their dinners, while
our troops reposed on the ground, apparently regardless of the presence of their enemy. During
this interval likewise, the wounded on both sides
were conveyed to the rear. From the closeness
of the engagement, they lay intermingled on the
field; and while engaged in this humane and
peaceful duty, a friendly intercourse took place
between the French and English soldiers; and,
shaking hands, they mutually expressed admiration of the gallantry displayed by their opponents.
About one o'clock, it became evident from several
heavy clouds of dust, that the enemy's columns
were again advancing. At two the work of havoc
re-commenced with a heavy cannonade, followed
by a general attack on the whole front of our line.
The enemy's infantry came on in four distinct
columns, covered by their light-troops, while their
cavalry, drawn up in rear, waited only for the
first appearance of confusion to complete the victory by an overwhelming charge. Notwithstanding the destruction which the French artillery occasioned in the ranks, our troops did not open fire
till the close approach of the columns enabled
them to do so with effect. That on the right un-

der Gen. Sebastiani, was suffered nearly to reach
the summit of the hill crowned by the redoubt, before any obstruction was made to their progress.
A heavy fire was at length opened by Gen. Campbell's brigade, and two Spanish battalions, posted
on the height. Our troops then charged, and in
gallant style drove the enemy before them; and
carrying a battery; took thirteen pieces of cannon.
The broken column, however, having rallied, was
again advancing, when it was charged in flank by
a Spanish regiment of cavalry, and compelled
once more to retreat in confusion. In the meantime, two columns on the enemy's right, consisting of Ruffin's and Villatte's divisions, supported
by cavalry again endeavored to gain possession of
the hill on the left. They were directed to support the attack on the front, by marching along
the bottom of the ravine, and turning the flank of
the position; while a body of light-troops, by a
wide movement across the mountains, were to
threaten an advance on the rear. To watch the
movements of the latter, a body of Spanish light-
infantry were moved into the valley in rear of the
left of the position. These formidable preparations for the attack of what was unquestionably
the most important point in the whole position,
naturally excited apprehensions for its safety.
The conical shape of the hill did not admit of its
being occupied by any considerable body of troops,
and Sir Arthur Wellesley determined to derange,

if possible, the combinations of the enemy by a charge of cavalry. Gen. Anson's brigade, consisting of the 23d light-dragoons and the first regiment of German hussars, supported by the heavy cavalry under Gen. Fane, were accordingly ordered to charge the enemy's column,, at the moment when emerging from the valley, they should attempt to deploy. These regiments advanced with great gallantry, regardless of the fire of several battalions of infantry. Unfortunately, the front of the enemy was protected by a deep ravine which had not been perceived, and which was found impassable for many of the horses. Confusion ensued in consequence. A considerable body of the 23d, however, led by Major Ponsonby, succeeded in crossing it, and passing between the divisions of Ruffin and Villatte, fell with irresistible impetuosity on two regiments of mounted chasseurs, which at once gave way. The 23d was then charged by some regiments in reserve, surrounded, broken and almost destroyed. A few only escaped, (among whom was Lord William Russel,) by passing at full speed through the intervals of the French columns. This charge was the only unfortunate occurrence of the day. It was ill-timed and injudicious. The ground had not been reconnoitered. Sir Arthur Wellesley's intention was that the cavalry should charge when the enemy by deploying, had extended and exposed their flank. When the charge was actually made,

the enemy were still in column, and too strongly
posted to afford any prospect of success. Yet notwithstanding its failure, the French were so as-
tonished at the boldness and gallantry of the attempt, as to desist from all farther efforts to gain
possession of the hill; and this imposing movement, which at first threatened the safety of the
whole army, was in effect attended by no important result. In the meanwhile the whole corps of
Marshal Victor advanced against the centre. One
column, composed chiefly of Germans, deployed on
the level ground before they attempted to assail
the position. The point selected for attack was
immediately on the right of the ground occupied
by General Hill's position, which formed the extreme left of the line. On the first indication of
the enemy's intention, Gen. Sherbrooke gave orders that his division should prepare for the charge.
The assailants came on, over the rough and broken ground in the valley, with great resolution,
and in the most imposing regularity, and were
encountered by our troops with their usual firmness. The whole division, as if moved by one
powerful and undivided impulse, advanced to meet
them; and pouring in a most galling and destructive fire, their ranks were speedily broken, and
they gave way. The impetuosity of the troops,
however, was not to be restrained; and the Guards,
having advanced too far in the ardor of pursuit,
were powerfully attacked in flank by the enemy's

reserve. The period was critical. In a few minutes the Guards had lost above five hundred of their number; their ranks were mowed down by the enemy's artillery; and the distruction of the whole brigade appeared inevitable. But the prescience of Sir Arthur Wellesley retrieved the army from the consequences of this misfortune. He had foreseen the danger to which the impetuosity of the Guards was likely to expose them, and ordered the 48th regiment and the cavalry under Gen. Cotton, to advance to their support. Under the cover thus afforded, the Guards, entirely broken, were able to effect their retreat. The enemy then directed their efforts against the 48th; but that regiment bravely stood its ground, till the Guards, again rallying, advanced with cheers to its support. The French then gave way, and were pursued for a considerable distance, though covered in their retreat, by a strong body of cavalry and artillery. Thus foiled at all points, the enemy withdrew their columns, and again concentrated on their position. But the fire of their artillery did not cease till dark. A dim and cheerless moon then rose, and threw a pallid lustre on the field, covered by the dying and the dead. Parties were sent out to bring in the wounded. The enemy were simililarly employed, and large fires were lighted along the whole front of his line. The loss of our army in this battle was severe; it amounted in killed, wounded and missing, to five thousand, three hundred and sixty-seven, and was occasioned chiefly by the close and well directed fire of the French artillery, which was kept up with little intermission throughout the day. Great as this amount of casualties unquestionably was, in an army whose numerical force did not exceed nineteen thousand men, it would have been incalculably greater, had not Sir Arthur Wellesley directed the different brigades to lie extended on the ground, behind the crest of the ridge, and only exposed them to the full action of the guns on the approach of the attacking columns. In this action, Major General Mackenzie, and Brig. Gen. Langworth, fell; Major General Hill and Major Gen. R. Campbell, were wounded.

The loss of the French, however, was much greater than that of the allies. It amounted to about ten thousand men. The loss of the Spaniards did not exceed twelve hundred and fifty in killed and wounded. The latter were only partially engaged; but the little which devolved on them to perform, was performed well. Their presence in position prevented a considerable body of the enemy from becoming disposable for attack on our troops. A body of Spanish artillery on the left was excellently served; and their cavalry made a gallant charge, which was entirely successful. In this battle I was severely wounded by the explosion of a bomb-shell, and was left as dead on the field, till the engagement was over. My

skull was factured, in consequence of which, I
have since suffered severely from the wound.
About six o'clock in the evening a dreadful occurrence took place.   The long dry grass took fire,
and the flames spreading rapidly over the field of
action, a great number of the wounded were
scorched to death.   For those who escaped, among
which I was happily numbered, a large hospital
was established in the town of Talavera.   During
the night, the soldies lay upon their arms, without
provisions of any kind.   It was expected that the
French would remain in their position, and renew
the battle in the morning.   But this anticipation
was not realized.   Under cover of the night they
retired, leaving in our hands twenty pieces of artillery.   One standard was taken, and one destroyed by the 29th regiment.   At daybreak, the rear
guard, consisting of cavalry was alone visible.
In the course of the 29th the army was reinforced
by the arrival of a troop of horse-artillery, and a
brigade of light-troops from Lisbon, under Gen.
Crawford.   Under the circumstances of his situation, however, it was impossible for Sir Auther
Wellesly to follow up his victory.   The position
he occupied was still one of extreme peril.   A
powerful enemy was advancing on his rear, and
no reliance could be placed for the supply of his
army, on the promises of the Spanish General, or
of the Junta.   But I cannot dwell on the partic-
ulars of his retreat, it would swallow up this little

work too soon, so I shall pass on to the next engagement, in which I took part.

After the capture of Cindad Rodrigo by Massenna, the enemy advanced against Almeida. Fort Conception was blown up at their approach; and Gen. Crawford with the light division, to which my regiment belonged, took post with his left flank resting on the fortress, and his right on the high ground above Val de Mula. Lord Wellington had directed that officer to avoid any engagement with the enemy, and on their approach, to fall back across the Coa. Gen. Crawford, however determined to await the arrival of the French columns, and not to retire till pressed by superior numbers. On the morning of 24th of July, the piquets were driven in by the French skirmishers which covered the advance of their columns. A vigorous attack was then made on our position, in which the whole corps of Ney was engaged. Our troops were compelled by superior numbers to give ground, and retreated down the hill to the Coa. From the rains the river was unfordable, and some confusion took place in crossing the bridge. The rear guard had to sustain a violent attack, and the French endeavored to push a body of cavalry across the stream; but the opposite bank of the Coa being precipitate, and occupied both by infantry and artillery, the attempt, though repeatedly made, was unsuccessful. Nor were the enemy's attempts to gain possession of the bridge more fortunate in result. Our troops who were posted behind walls, which formed a kind of natural retrenchment for their defence, kept up so warm a fire on the assailants, that they were uniformly repulsed, notwithstanding their great numerical superiority; and General Crawford, having maintained his new position till evening, fell back under cover of the night. The loss of our division in this honorable engagement amounted to thirty killed and two hundred and seventy wounded. Among the former was my own gallant Colonel Hull of the 43d, whose loss was much lamented. In this engagement a musket ball struck my knapsack, went through my great-coat and blanket, and through a piece of bent leather that we carry for soles, and into my shaving dish, and lodged there, breaking the glass. It did not sound in the least like a shot, but on examination I found it was.

The next movement of the enemy was directed against Almeida, a fortress garrisoned by four thousand Portuguese, under the command of Col. Cox; which after a brave resistance surrendered to Massena. The fall of Almeida left no farther obstacle to the enemy's advance, and on the 16th September, having been joined by the corps of Gen. Regnier-Massena commenced his march into Portugal. Wellington still kept retiring along the left bank of the Mondego, strengthening both his numbers and position, as the enemy gradually advanced. Having ascertained the direction of the enemy's march to be towards Portuguese Estramadura, he immediately occupied the heights of Busaco. The position thus occupied consisted of one lofty ridge, extending from the Mondego northward for a distance of about eight miles. It attains an elevation of two hundred and fifty feet above the ground immediately in front, and is covered by gorges and defiles of extreme difficulty. Its principal disadvantage as a position, lay in its extent, which was manifestly too great to admit of its being occupied at all points by an army not above sixty thousand strong. Some skirmishing had occurred on the twenty-third between our division and the advanced guard of the French. We distroyed the bridge across the Criz, on the road to Coimbra; but, on the following day the river was passed by the leading divisions of the enemy, and on the 26th, the whole French army was concentrated in front of the British position. Even at this period, Massena seems to have formed no just appreciation of the skill and activity of his opponent. He had calculated on deranging his schemes, by the rapidity of his march, and imagined it impossible that the army should have been joined by the corps of Gen. Hill. On reconnoitering the position, therefore, he considered its extent too great to admit of successful defence, and is said to have observed to one of the unworthy Portuguese by whom he was surrounded. "I cannot persuade myself that Lord Wellington will risk the loss of his reputation by giving battle; but if he does, I have him ! To-morrow, we shall effect the conquest of Portugal, and in a few days, I shall drown the Leopard !"

The head quarters of Lord Wellington were fixed in the Convent of.La Trappe, which crowns the Serra. From that elevated position, indeed from the whole summit of the height, the French army were distinctly visible. No sight could be more beautiful and striking. The eye rested on a vast multitude of men, clad in the imposing panoply of war—their arms glittering in the sun—standards waving in the air, while the distant sound of the trumpet or bugle loaded the breeze.

BATTLE OF BUSACO.

On the evening of the 26th of September, the line of battle was formed. The division of Gen. Hill, with those of Leith and Picton on his left, occupied the right of the position.

The first division under Sir Brent Spencer was in the centre, General Cole's on the left. Our division was advanced somewhat in front of the left and centre. The main body of the cavalry under Sir Stapleton Cotton formed in the plains in front of Mealhada, and across the Oporto road ; and the brigade of Gen. Fane remained on the left bank of the Mondego, to repel any reconnoisance which the enemy might attempt in that direction.

Such was the distribution of the allied army. Day-dawn on the 27th, showed the enemy drawn up for immediate attack. The corps of Ney was form-ed in close column opposite to the Convent of Bu-saco. That of Regnier appeared in front of Pic-ton's division, prepared to advance by the road crossing the height St. Antonio de Cantara. Ju-not's corps was in reserve, with the greater part of the cavalry, and was posted on some rising ground about a mile in rear of Marshal Ney. In this order, covered by his light-troops, the enemy's columns moved on to the attack. The abruptness and inequalities of the ascent contributed to cover their advance, and they reached the summit of the ridge without more serious opposition, than the occasional fire of guns posted on the flanking points. It was with the corps of Regnier, that the first hostile collision took place. The regiments in the part of the line to which he penetrated, had not reached the position assigned to them, and for a moment the height was in possession of the en-emy. Their leading battalions were in the act of deploying into line, when Gen. Picton, at the head of a few companies hastily collected, came up, and with these, and the light troops, he kept the enemy in play, until joined by the 8th Portuguese regiment commanded by Major Birmingham, when charging the enemy's column in flank, he drove them in great confusion down the hill, and across the ravine. About a mile on the right, the enemy

made strenuous efforts to gain possession of the
pass of St. Antonio. These however were defeated by the 74th regiment, and a brigade of Portuguese, directed by Colonel Mackinnon, who, without assistance was enabled to maintain his post
in spite of every effort to dislodge him. Notwithstanding the complete discomfiture of his first attack by General Picton, on the left of the pass,
the enemy's column still continued to press forward, and again reached the summit of the height.
From this the 88th regiment under Col. Wallace,
and four companies of the 45th, dislodged them
by a gallant charge ; and a brigade of General
Leith's division, coming up at the same moment,
the enemy were borne down the hill with irresistible impetuosity, and desisted from all farther attempt on this part of the position. The attack of
Ney was even less successful. With a division of
his corps found in column of mass, he advanced
against the height occupied by our (the light) division. General Pack's brigade of Portuguese
were also placed here, and we were ordered to
change coats with them in order to deceive the
enemy. During his advance, the enemy experienced little opposition, and without difficulty
gained possession of a village situated on the
brow of the ascent; but, no sooner did he crown
the height, then he found us drawn up to receive
him, and his column became exposed to a most
destructive fire, both of musketry and artillery.

This however was but of short duration, yet, so long, that the leading regiments of the assailants were almost totally annihilated. A charge of bayonets followed; the whole column was routed, and driven down the hill with prodigous slaughter. We pursued them into the village, when we were stopped by some artillery which they had there in reserve. While endeavoring to regain the hill, I ran into a house which was deserted, in order to avoid their fire, for a moment, and while there, I observed the end of a sword hanging from the chimney just below the jamb. Thinking there must be an owner to it, I looked up the chimney and discovered a French officer, who had hid there to escape pursuit. I immediately pulled him down and told him that he was my prisoner, upon which he took out a gold watch and gave it to me if I would release him. I immediately took the watch, and was leaving in a hurry, when unfortunately for the Frenchman, I met another soldier at the door, who however consented to let him go upon his giving him his gold epaulets.

A very curious incident occurred before we charged the enemy upon the ascent. While they were advancing up the hill, a field-officer was observed upon a very fine horse at a short distance from the main body. A private of our regiment by the name of Carroll, asked permission from his Captain, to go out and take possession of the officer's horse. The Captain readily gave him permission, though laughing at the idea, and the soldier sprang out of the ranks towards the enemy, waving his shako upon his bayonet. The enemy surprised, and thinking that perhaps he was the bearer of some message, or something of the kind, did not fire upon him, and running up to the officer, as if about to communicate something, he seized him by the leg, and being a very strong, man, threw him instantly upon the ground. Throwing himself quickly upon the horse he rode back into our ranks, amid the cheers of his comrades.

At about eight o'clock in the morning, a fog came on, which, for a time, particularly obscured the positions of the two armies; when the day cleared, however, it was discovered that the French had placed large bodies of light troops in the woods which skirted the bottom of the Serra. In consequence, a continued skirmishing took place during the day. It was probably the intention of Massena, by this manoeuvre, to draw Lord Wellington into an engagement of some consequence, in a situation where the advantage of position should be less decidedly in his favor. But Lord Wellington was immovable. He advanced the brigade of Col. Pakenham to the support of the light troops, but directed them to retire when pressed, leaving his position again open to the enemy, should he think proper to attack it. Massena however, was but little inclined to avail himself of the facility thus afforded. The day passed without farther attack on our position, and on the approach of night, the French retired from the ground they had occupied during the day, and our division again took possession of the village from which they had been driven in the morning. The loss of the French army in this engagement amounted to between five and six thousand men, including four General officers, one of whom, (Graindorge) was killed; another, (Simon) wounded and made prisoner. Our loss and that of the Portuguese did not amount to twelve hundred men. After this victory, Lord Wellington evacuated the position of Busaco, and retreated to the banks of the Tagus and Torres Vedras, and suffered Massena to take possession of Coimbra without a struggle. The French General having removed to Santarem, a city on a hill near the Tagus, the British commander resolved to attack this post, which he hoped to find only defended by a rear guard. In this however he was mistaken; the hostile troops were numerous, and, from their situation every way prepared to offer a successful resistance. He accordingly withdrew his forces, and established his head quarters at Artaxo, after which the armies on both sides remained for a season inactive. Such was the situation of affairs in Portugal at the close of the year 1810, when, although no decisive victory had been obtained over the French, they had, nevertheless, been foiled in some

of their principal movements, and had failed in
their boast of placing the eagles of Napoleon upon the tower of Lisbon.

On the 5th of March 1811, the French evacuated Santarem, which was occupied by the allied
armies next day ; and a pursuit of the enemy was
shortly afterwards commenced. Massena however
managed his retreat in so masterly a manner, that
Wellington found it difficult to embarrass him.
At length the former made a halt at Pombal, but
left town in the night, and thus escaped the attack of the latter, who had brought up his troops
with all possible expedition in front of his adversary. In two days afterwards he came into action
with Ney, at Redinha, and forced him to retire by
the bridge and ford of that place. He then pushed
on for Condeixa, to prevent if possible the passage
of the Mondego, by Massena ; and such was the
rapidity of the British in effecting this movement,
that Massena was very nearly taken and had to
scramble over the mountains at night, to regain
his head quarters at Ponte Cobuta. At length
however he determined on a final effort to maintain himself within the frontier, by posting his
army in a strong position along the banks of the
Coa. Their right flank extended to Ruivina,
guarding the ford of Raponla de Coa, with a detachment at the bridge of Ferrereas. The left
was at Subugal, and the eighth corps at Alfayates.
The right of the allied army was opposite Subu-

gal, the left at the bridge of Ferrereas; and Trant and Wilson crossed the Coa below Almeida, to threaten the communication of that place with Ciudad Rodrigo and the French army. The enemy was posted so strongly that his position was only approachable by the left flank; and on themorning of the third of April, our division was directed to cross the Coa at a ford several miles above Subugal, in rear of the corps of Regnier, while the third and fifth divisions should attack him in front, the latter crossing the river at the bridge of Subugal, the former at a ford a short distance above it. The sixth division remained opposite to Ruivina, and a battalion of the seventh observed their detachment at the bridge of Ferrereas. The day was dark and cloudy, and a deep mist occasionaly overspread the horizon, accompanied by storms of rain, which narrowed the scope of vision to the distance of a yard or two. A part of our division had already crossed the river, when one of these impervious fogs came on. The enemy's piquets were driven in, and the troops advancing in pursuit, came at unawares on the left of the main body of Regnier's corps, which it was intended they should turn. The consequence was that the advance was driven back on my own, the 43d regiment; and Regnier by a partial dissipation of the mist, having ascertained the smallness of the force opposed to him, directed on it a strong column of infantry supported by artillery and horse.

This attack encountered a spirited repulse ; and Colonel Beckwith's brigade advanced in turn against the enemy's position, where they were attacked by a fresh column of infantry on the left, and by a regiment of cavalry on the right. In this charge, twenty-seven men of my own company were cut down, thirteen of whom were killed, and the others, myself among the number, wounded. Under these circumstances the leading battalion would probably been sacrificed, had not Colonel Beckwith, with great promptitude, retreated behind some stone enclosures, which enabled him to maintain his ground. The combat was then waged with vigor and pertinacity on both sides. Colonel Beckwith's brigade made another charge, drove back the enemy, and had gained possession of a howitzer, when the French cavalry advancing on our flank, again forced us to retire to our post. There we were joined by the other brigade of the light division, and Colonel Beckwith again advanced with his own brigade, and the first battalion of the fifty-second. We were once more charged in flank by a fresh column of infantry supported by cavalry, and Colonel Beckwith took post in an enclosure on the top of the height, which enabled him to protect the howitzer, in the capture of which so much gallantry had been displayed. In this state of things, when Regnier was disposing his troops for another attack, the head of Picton's division came up, and immediately opened fire. At the same moment the fifth division under General Dunlop, having forced the bridge, was seen ascending the heights to the enemy's right, and the cavalry appeared on the high ground in rear of the left. Regnier then observing himself to be nearly surrounded, retreated with great precipitation to Alfayates, leaving the howitzer and above three hundred men dead on the field. About an equal number were made prisoners. Our loss in killed, wounded and missing, amounted to one hundred and sixty-one.

Considering the great numerical disparity of the parties, in this well-fought engagement, the conduct of our division was admirable. Under circumstances of disadvantage, impossible to be foreseen, they maintained a contest of the most unequal description, and executed their manœuvers in the presence of a superior enemy, with the most imposing steadiness and precision. "Although the operations of this day," says Lord Wellington, " were by unavoidable accidents, not performed in the manner I intended they should have been, I consider the action that was fought by the light division—by Colonel Beckwith's brigade principally—to be one of the most glorious that British troops were ever engaged in." Had the retreat of Regnier not been favored by the fog, the results of the engagement would have been yet more brilliant and decisive. The cavalry continued the pursuit as far as Alfayates, at which place the

whole French army crossed the frontier and entered Spain.   Massena hastened to concentrate behind the Agueda, and on the eighth of April not a
Frenchman remained in Portugal, except the gar
rison of Almeida, for the blockade of which Lord
Wellington made immediate preparations.   Our
army then took up a position on the Duas Casas,
with its advanced posts on Gallegos and the
Agueda. The militia under Trant and Wilson were
at Cinca Villas and Malpartido ; and the communication of Almeida, both with Ciudad Rodigo,
and with the French army, was cut off.

Thus terminated the invasion of Portugal ; that
invasion by which it was boastingly predicted that
the British would be driven into the sea, and the
conquest of Portugal be decisively achieved.

BATTLE OF ALBUERA,
May 16, 1811.

Regent Blake hearing that operations were successful in Portugal, effected a junction with Castanos, and having had an interview with Marshal
Beresford at Valverde, it was agreed to offer battle to the enemy.   Our army accordingly took post
on the heights of Albuera.   The ground we occupied was a chain of eminences, along the front of
which flowed the river Albuera, a narrow stream
and fordable in many places above the position.
Towards the left, the great road from Serville, leads
over it by a bridge, and subsequently branches off

to Badajos and Olivenca. On the left of this road, and a short distance from the bridge, stands the village of Albuera, containing a church and about one hundred houses, which had been deserted by their inhabitants. Below the bridge the Albuera was unfordable. The western bank occupied by the allies was of considerable altitude, and commanded all the ground to the eastward. The right of the position, from its height, could not be well occupied.

On the evening of the 15th, the leading division of the French army took part on some wooded ground, about a mile distant, which stretched in a semicircular sweep downward to the river. The remainder came up during the night, and Soult, with a force of eighteen thousand infantry, four thousand cavalry, and forty pieces of cannon found himself in the presence of his enemy.

The allied army was somewhat superior in numbers. It consisted of a corps of twelve thousand Spaniards, which joined during the night; of thirteen thousand British and Portuguese infantry, two thousand cavalry, and thirty-two guns.

Beresford occupied his position in the following manner:—The Spaniards were posted on the right in two lines, their left terminating on the Valverde road, where it joined the right of General Stewart's division which occupied the centre. Gen. Hamilton's Portuguese division was on the left, supported by a brigade of German light infantry,

which held the village of Albuera. Gen. Cole's
division which only came up as the action commenced, and one brigade of Gen. Hamilton's division, formed a second line in rear of the left and
centre,   A strong body of artillery was posted for
the protection of the bridge, and the cavalry under General Lumley, lent support to the Spaniards
on the right.

On the morning of the 16th of May, about 8
o'clock, the French army were observed to be in
motion ; and shortly afterwards, a strong force of
cavalry, supported by two columns of infantry
and several guns, issued from the wooded ground
between the Ferdia, and the Albuera, and directed its march towards the bridge. The artillery
immediately opened fire, and a heavy cannonade
was kept up on both sides, with great effect on
the part of the British, from their advantages of
ground.   In the mean time, Soult crossing the Albuera under cover of the wood, above the position,
advanced with the main body of his army, and
without opposition took possession of the heights
on the right flank of the Spaniards. The combat
then commenced. The Spanish troops, after a
short resistance, were driven from their ground,
and Soult then formed his army in a line, extending to the Velverde road, and raking that of the
allies.

It became instantly essential to the safety of
the army, that the enemy should be driven from

the commanding station he had thus assumed. Beresford gave new directions ; Gen. Cole's division was placed in an oblique line, with its right flank thrown back, and an endeavor was made to bring up the Spanish troops to the charge. This failed. A heavy fire was kept up by the French artillery, and a charge of cavalry again forced them to retire in great confusion. General Stewart's division, therefore was brought up, and passing through the Spaniards, advanced to gain possession of the heights. At this period a storm of rain came on, which completely darkened the atmosphere, and rendered it impossible to discern the movements of the enemy at any distance. The right brigade, under Col. Colburne, consisting of the Buffs, the sixty-sixth, the second battalion, forty-eighth, and the thirty-first, was in the act of deploying, the two leading battalions alone having completed the manœuvre, when a regiment of Polish lancers, which under shelter of the mist had circled their flank, made furious charge from the rear. The result was, that the whole brigade with the exception of the thirty-first, which still remained in column, were driven forward into the enemy's line and made prisoners.

General Latour Maubourg, then took post beyond the right of the allies, waiting for the first indication of retreat, to execute a grand and decisive charge, and throw confusion into the movement. Their motions were watched by the heavy

brigade under General Lumley, and the horse artillery did considerable execution in their ranks.

It was under such circumstances that the brigade of General Houghton was advanced to retrieve
if possible the fortunes of the day.   A contest of
the most bloody and pertinacious character, ensued.   The leading regiment, the twenty-ninth, no
sooner reached the summit of the heights, than it
was assailed by a fire of musquetry and artillery,
which spread havoc through the ranks, and in leading this regiment to the charge, General Houghton
fell pierced with wounds.   Unfortunately the in-
tervention of a steep but narrow gully, rendered
it impossible to reach the enemy with the bayonet,
and the twenty-ninth was directed to halt and
open fire.   The fifty-seventh and forty-eighth, then
came up, and assuming their position in line, the
struggle was maintained on both sides with desperate courage.

In this state of things General Cole directed the
Fusileer brigade to advance on the enemy's left
and ascend the disputed heights from the valley.
In the execution of this movement, General Cole,
and almost every individual attached to his staff
were wounded.   The Fusileer brigade, on crown-
ing the ascent, was received with a fire so tremendous, that it at first recoiled, but instantly recovering its ground, displayed throughout the remainder of this desperate conflict, a degree of
steadiness and intrepidity impossible to be sur-

passed. Col. Sir William Myers, commanding the brigade, was killed early in the action, and his country was thus deprived of the services of a most gallant and accomplished officer.

General Houghton's brigade maintained its ground in spite of all the enemy's effort to dislodge it. Above two-thirds of its numbers had fallen, and yet not one inch of ground had been yielded; at length for the want of ammunition it retired with the most perfect regularity. The French were forced from their position with immense slaughter and retired across the Albuera.

About three o'clock the firing had entirely ceased, and both armies took post on the ground they had occupied in the morning. Thus terminated one of the most fierce and murderous contests which took place during the war. Out of seven thousand five hundred British, four thousand one hundred and fifty-eight were killed, wounded or missing. The total loss of the allies, in the engagement amounted to nearly seven thousand men.

Wellington narrowly escaped being drowned in attempting to swim his horse across the Duero.*

This leads me to the Battle of Fuentes and capture of Almeida.

* His orderly who accompanied him was carried down the stream with the current and drowned.

BATTLE OF FUENTES AND CAPTURE OF ALMEIDA.

On the 28th of April, Lord Wellington established his head quarters at Villa Formosa. The
numerical strength of the enemy amounted to forty thousand infantry, and five thousand cavalry,
while Wellington could only muster an effective
force of thirty six thousand men, of which not more
than two thousand were cavalry. Notwithstanding this disparity, he determined to oppose Massena in his attempt to relieve Almeida ; and accordingly concentrated his army to give battle.

Almeida stands on the right of the Coa, a river
of considerable magnitude, which from the steep-
ness of its banks, affords few points at which it
can be crossed by an army. The bridge immediately in rear of Almeida is within range of the
guns of the fortress, and at the period in question
was so dilapidated as to be nearly impassable.
There is another at Castello Bom, about two
leagues above Almeida ; but this also was a most
difficult communication. A little higher up there
is a ford but between that point and Sabugal, the
river cannot be crossed. At the latter place, the
road from Ciudad Rodrigo leads across a stone
bridge, affording the only safe and convenient
communication in case of retreat.

Lord Wellington, therefore, was naturally anxious to adopt a position which should enable him

at once to protect the approach to Almeida, and cover this important line of communication. He was fully aware, however, that the great extension of front thus rendered necessary, was highly disadvantageous ; and, from the first, he contemplated the probability of being forced by circumstances to relinquish the communication by Sabugal, and concentrate his army in a more confined position, for the protection of Almeida alone.

Between the Duas Casas and the Touron rivers, both of which run nearly parallel to the Coa, is a range of easy heights, along which Lord Wellington formed the centre of his army. In front of these is the village of Fuentes d'Honore, which, though not strictly speaking embraced in the position, was held as an advanced post, and contributed materially to its strength. General Houston with the seventh division, was posted on the extreme right of the lines, and a body of Spanish cavalry, under Don Julian Sanchez, was placed in the village of Nava d'Aver about two miles beyond it, to add to the security which that flank derived from the extreme difficulty of the ground in its rear of Fuentes d'Honore, their light infantry occupying the village. The sixth and light divisions were posted in rear of Almada, where the Duas Casas is crossed by a bridge. The fifth division formed the extreme left of the line, and guarded the great road to Almeida, with its flank resting on Fort Conception. The Portuguese bri-

gade of General Pack, supported by a British battalion, was employed in blockading Almeida. On
the third of May, the enemy appeared in front of
the position, and took post on a ridge which over-
hangs the village of Fuentes d'Honore, nearly parallel to that occupied by the allies. A brisk skirmish took place between the light troops, followed by a heavy cannonade, and a desperate attack
on the village. Lieutenant-Colonel Williams, with
the light-infantry battalions of the first and third
divisions, maintained this post with great gallantry and resolution; but fresh numbers of the enemy,
pouring on to the attack, it was found necessary
to support him successively with the seventy-first,
the seventy-ninth, and the twenty-fourth regiments.
The contest was continued on both sides with great
obstinacy and perseverance, till the approach of
night, when the assailants repulsed in all their efforts, took advantage of the darkness to retire.

On the morning of the 5th, the French army
were observed to have made a general movement;
and the corps of Junot, with all the cavalry, appeared in two columns, on the opposite side of the
valley of the Duas Casas, in front of Poco Velho.
Wellington, in consequence, sent the light division
and the cavalry to the support of Gen. Houston,
and the first and third divisions also made a movement to their right.

About seven o'clock the enemy drove in the advanced guard of the British, and took possession

of the village of Poco Velho. The cavalry under
General Montbrun, having driven Don Julian
Sanchez from Nava d'Aver, now executed a general charge, supported by infantry and guns, and
forced the British cavalry to retire in some confusion.

Though this attack was repulsed, the numerous
cavalry of the enemy were observed to be collecting on the right flank, while large masses of infantry were forming in front. Under these circumstances, Lord Wellington decided on with-
drawing his army to a more concentrated position,
and giving up the communication by Sabugal.
The seventh and light divisions were directed to
retire, and a new alignment was taken up, extending from the Duas Casas to the Turon, nearly
at right angles with that in which the army had
hitherto been formed. The seventh division was
posted on a height beyond the Turon, which commanded the whole plain to Frenada ; and the cavalry and light division, to which I was attached,
were directed to form in reserve, in rear of the
left of the first division.

This retrogressive movement was executed with
the most perfect regularity, though pressed by the
enemy's cavalry, which strongly supported by artillery, made repeated charges on the retiring divisions. During this movement the Chasseurs
Brittanniques in particular, distinguished themselves. They repulsed a furious charge ; and by

a well directed flanking fire, compelled the French to retire with considerable loss. The conduct of the horse-artillery, under Captain Bull was also admirable. Nothing could exceed the skill and boldness with which it was manœuvred ; and thus supported, the infantry accomplished its retrogression in unbroken order, and with a loss far inferior to that of the enemy.

When the division reached their gound, the cavalry, in pushing through the intervals of the new alignment, occasioned some confusion ; and taking instant advantage of this circumstance, General Montbrun ordered his whole cavalry to charge. In order to protect the retiring division, the line of march had been flanked by two brigades of guns, which instantly opened fire on the approach of the enemy. The infantry likewise poured in several volleys ; and, thus severely handled, the French cavalry retreated in confusion, and Montbrun desisted from further effort.

In the meanwhile the sixth corps, which during these events remained opposite to Fuentes d'Honore, had made strenuous efforts to gain possession of that important post. About nine in the morning, several brigades of artillery were brought opposite to the village, and pointed in readiness to fire. At length on a given signal, the whole of their guns opened fire on the village, and several columns of infantry moved forward to the attack.

A struggle of the fiercest and most obstinate character ensued. The seventy-first, seventy-ninth, and twenty-fourth regiments defended the village with the greatest gallantry, disputing every inch of ground. In this state of things, Colonel Cameron of the seventy-ninth, commanding the brigade, was killed, and the enemy continuing to pour in fresh columns, at length succeeded in overpowing the defenders. No sooner however did the assailants attempt to form beyond the houses, than the eighty-eighth, seventy-fourth and eighty-third regiments, advancing to the charge, drove them back into the village with the bayonet, where the contest re-commenced, and continued to be kept up on both sides, with great vigour and obstinacy, till the streets may be said literally to have been covered with blood.

Towards evening the fire on both sides gradually slackened, and the village as if by mutual consent, was divided by the combatants, the upper part being occupied by our troops, the lower by the enemy. The result of these repeated efforts convinced Massena that he had nothing to hope from continuing the contest. During the whole of the sixth an unbroken tranquility reigned in both armies, and on the morning of the seventh he withdrew his troops from the front of our position. The loss of our army in the actions of the third and fifth, amounted to about seventeen hundred men. That of the enemy, from their acting

throughout as assailants, must have been considerable greater. In the village of Fuentes, the
lanes, the church, the court-yards, and the gardens
were found literally piled with the dying and the
dead. We made likewise a considerable number
of prisoners. Wellington now marched to meet
Soult, who was in motion for Estramadura, and,
shortly afterwards, had the gratification of hearing that Massena had so far despaired of success,
as to resign the command of the army of Portugal to Marshal Marmont. On the nineteenth of
May, he reached Elvas, where he received intelligence of the battle of Albuera. He also learned
that the the investment of Badajos had been renewed on the same day, and that Soult was in full
retreat towards Seville, followed by the allied
cavalry, Lord Wellington then immediately assumed the personal directions of the operations
against Badajos; but after loosing five hundred
men in the vain attempt to scale the walls, he
thought it prudent to raise the siege. He now
turned his attention to Ciudad Rodrigo; and, having established his head quarters at Fuente Guin-
aldo, he sent his battering train and stores from
the Tagus to the Douro, and watched for a favorable opportunity of advancing against Rodrigo.

On the sixth of January, 1812, in the following
year, Wellington prepared to commence his long
meditated attack on Ciudad Rodrigo.

SIEGE OF CIUDAD RODRIGO.

Accordingly head quarters were transferred from
Frenada to Gallegos; but the [ground being covered with snow, and the weather inclement, the
army did not move till the eighth. Our division
alone crossed the Agueda, and formed the investment; but the other divisions took part in all the
duties of the siege, and were prepared, if necessary, to move to the support of the investing force.
Shortly after dark, on the same evening, parties
from the third, fourth, and light divisions broke
ground before the fortress, under a heavy fire;
and a redoubt, situated on the great Teson, was
gallantly stormed by a party of the light division,
of which my own company formed a part, under
Lieut. Col. Colburne. The immediate direction of
the siege was entrusted to Sir Thomas Graham,
who had succeeded Sir Brent Spencer as second in
command. By the capture of the redoubt, a powerful preliminary obstacle to the operations of the
besiegers was removed. On the night following,
the first parallel was established, and the batteries traced out. On the night of the thirteenth, a
fortified convent, situated on the right of the redoubt, was attacked and carried by a detachment
of light infantry companies supported by Lord
Blantyre's brigade. The assailants succeeded in
approaching the convent unobserved; and, effecting an entrance, took the garrison by surprise. As

this post was of considerable importance, a lodgment was formed in it, and the sap was carried
on to the line of the second parallel.   On the fourteenth, the garrison took advantage of a moment
when the trenches were unguarded, to make a
sortie.   By a culpable negligence, the guard, quitting the trenches, were accustomed to depart on
observing the approach of the relief.   For a moment therefore, the enemy were successful; the
workmen, armed only with spade and mattock,
hastily retired; but the alarm was instantly given,
and the assailants were driven back, without effecting more injury than that of upsetting a few
gabions into the sap.   In the meanwhile, intelligence was received that Marmont, ignorant of the
operations of the allies, was approaching, with the
view of throwing supplies into the place.   But as
this ignorance could be but of short duration,
Lord Wellington determined to push forward his
advances with the utmost rapidity, in the hope of
carrying the town, before Marmont and Dorsenne
should be enabled to collect their forces for its relief.   In case, however, he should be defeated in
this object, preparations were made for encoun-
tering the combined army in the field.   The divisions in the more distant cantonments, were
moved up to the neighborhood of Ciudad Rodrigo;
and General Hill was directed to throw two brigades across the Tagus, to move as occasion might
require.

It was considered of importance to gain possession of the Convent of St. Francisco, by which the
approaches were enfiladed on the left. Batteries
were accordingly erected against it, which speedily
destroyed, the defences, and on the night of the fourteenth it was carried by assault. The second parallel was then completed, and progress made by sap
towards the crest of the glacis. Advances were
likewise made from the left of the first parallel
down the slope of the hill, and fresh batteries established, from which an incessant fire was kept
up on the *fausse braie,* and body of the place. On
the nineteenth two practicable breaches were completed, one in the *fausse braie,* the other in the
main wall, and preparations immediately made
for storming them, though the sap had not been
brought to the crest of the glacis, and the counterscarp of the ditch was still entire. The attack
of the main breach was committed to the division
of General Picton, consisting of the brigade of
Major General Mackinnon and Lieutenant-Colonel
Campbell. The column was to be preceded by a
storming party, consisting of the light companies
of the division under Major Manners of the seventy-fourth ; and, to divert the attention of the garrison, a demonstration was to be made on the right,
by Lieutenant-Colonel O'Toole, with five companies of the ninety-fifth rifle corps, and the light companies of the eighty-third and ninety-fourth. Our
division consisting of the brigades of Major-Gen-

eral Vandeleur and Colonel Barnard, was directed to assault the smaller breach, headed by a
storming party or forlorn hope of three hundred
men, led by Major Napier of the fifty-second regiment. This party, to which I belonged were
volunteers. General Pack was instructed to make
a false attack with his brigade on the outwork of
St. Iago, and the Convent of La Caridada, with
instructions to convert it into a real one, should
circumstances prove favorable. Soon after dark.
on the nineteenth, the troops were under arms,
and at seven o'clock advanced to the assault. In
order to facilitate the advance of the main storming party under General Mackinnon, and remove
such impediments as the enemy might oppose to
their ascent of the main breach, Colonel Campbell, with the ninety-fourth regiment, and second
battalion of the fifth which had been placed as
near as possible to the town, descended the counterscarp, by means of ropes, and moved silently to
the breach, which they succeeded in reaching
without discovery. Not meeting with any serious
obstacle to retard their progress, and aware of the
danger of delay at such a crisis, Colonel Campbell, on his own responsibility, formed the daring
resolution of storming the town, though such an
attempt was not warranted by his orders. At this
moment he could only avail himself of the battalion of the fifth and the right wing of the ninety-
fourth, but placing himself at their head, he in-

stantly commenced ascending the breach. The enemy were now on the alert; and Colonel Campbell had nearly reached the summit of the breach, when he distinctly heard the enemy's artillery men receive orders to fire. With great promptitude he instantly ordered the men to throw themselves flat on their faces. No sooner had this been done than a shower of shot and shells swept over them; and the troops, springing to their feet, again poured onward, and in a few moments the breach was cleared. In endeavoring to reach the ramparts on the right, an unexpected obstacle occurred. The enemy had cut a wide ditch between the breach and the ramparts; but here one of those fortunate incidents occurred on which the most important events frequently depend. Across the ditch two planks had been placed by the enemy, and in the confusion of their retreat, they had removed one of them, but neglected the other. Along this temporary bridge the troops passed to the ramparts on the right, driving the artillery men from the guns and carrying every thing before them. New difficulties however soon presented themselves. The storming party, under General Mackinnon, had not yet appeared; and the garrison, recovering from their panic, made a powerful attack on their assailants. Under these circumstances, Colonel Campbell ordered a volley, and then charging at the head of his detachment, the French immediately fled, throwing down their

arms. Such had been the celerity of Col. Campbell's movements, that when on the ramparts, his
men were fired at by the light-troops from without the town, who were ignorant of its having
been already stormed. It was at this period that
the column of General Mackinnon commenced its
attack. It was received by a shower of grape
and musquetry, which did great execution; but
the troops pressing onward, succeeded in clearing
the breach. Unfortunately an expense magazine
on the ramparts accidentally caught fire, and Gen.
Mackinnon and many of his followers were killed
by the explosion. Notwithstanding this misfortune, and a destructive fire kept up by the garrison from behind an interior retrenchment, the assailants maintained their ground, till the troops
which had already entered came to their assistance, when the enemy gave way. In the meanwhile, General Vandeleur's brigade of the light
division, which had formed behind the Convent
in the suburb, nearly opposite to the lesser breach,
advanced at the appointed moment to the assault.
General Crawford,—then whom the service boast-
ed no more zealous and accomplished officer—received his death wound on the glacis, while leading on his division; and General Vandeleur, Col.
Colburne, and Major George Napier who led the
storming party, were likewise wounded. The
courage of our soldiers, however was not daunted.
Notwithstanding the tremendous fire by which they

were assailed, the column continued its advance. The breach was carried in spite of every obstacle ; and having hastily formed, we swept round the ramparts to the larger breach.

The column of General Pack had likewise been successful in their escalade, and the town was carried at all points. The garrison fled in confusion, throwing away their arms, and the whole of the survivors were made prisoners. This successful achievment was followed by the usual scenes of riot and excess. The men, no longer amenable to discipline, ransacked the houses in search of plunder. In a storehouse I got my haversack full of silver plate, which the French had plundered from the churches. The cellars were broken open and emptied of their contents ; many houses were wantonly set on fire, and the yells of brutal triumph, uttered by the intoxicated soldiers, were heard in wild dissonance with the screams of the wounded. Thus passed the night. In the morning by the exertions of the officers, discipline was partially restored. The soldiers by degrees returned to their duty, and the blind appetites of their brutal nature became again subjected to moral restraint. The loss of our army in the siege and storming of Ciudad Rodrigo, was considerable, though not more than might have been anticipated in such an operation. It amounted to one thousand three hundred and ten men, in killed and wounded. Of the garrison, one thousand seven hundred were

made prisoners, and their loss in killed and wounded was estimated at a thousand. In the town were
found a battering train of forty-four pieces, an
immense quantity of ammunition, several thousand stand of arms, and considerable stores of provisions. The reduction of Ciudad Rodrigo was
was unquestionably an operation of great brilliance. It was effected in the depth of winter, with
a rapidity for which Marmont was altogether unprepared. On the arrival of the news in England,
Lord Wellington was made an Earl, and received the thanks of Parliament, which voted him an
additional income of two thousand pounds a year;
whilst in Spain his services were rewarded by the
title of Duke of Ciudad Rodrigo, with the rank of
a grandee of Spain of the first class.

SIEGE OF BADAJOS.

On the fall of Ciudad Rodrigo, Lord Wellington
determined on the bold project of throwing his
army with suddenness and secresy across the Tagus, and reducing Badajos before Soult and Marmont, should be able to take effective measures
for its relief. The success of the enterprise depended on secresy and rapidity of movement, and
every means were adopted by Lord Wellington, to
conceal his intentions from the enemy, till the last
moment. At length, the arrangements being completed, the army on the sixth of March broke up
from its quarters, and moving rapidly to the south,

reached Elvas on the eleventh. One division only covered by a few cavalry posts, remained on the Agueda. On the sixteenth of March, the army crossed the Guadiana, and Badajos was immediately invested by the third, fourth, and light divisions, under command of Marshal Beresford and General Picton, Sir Thomas Graham, with the first, sixth and seventh divisions of infantry, and General Slade's and General Le Marchant's brigades of cavalry, advanced to Los Santos, Zafra, and Llerena; and Sir Rowland Hill, with the second division, and the Portuguese division of General Hamilton, and one brigade of cavalry, moved from his cantonments near Albuquerque to Almandrelejo and Merida. General Dronet, part of whose corps was stationed at Villa Franca, finding himself thus threatened in front and flank, immediate-fell back to Hornachos. In the meantime the siege went on. On the seventeenth, the weather, which had hitherto been remarkably fine, became cold and tempestuous. During the afternoon and throughout the night the rain fell in torrents; and taking advantage of the obscurity, ground was broken within one hundred and sixty yards of Fort Picurina, undiscovered by the enemy. During the eighteenth, in spite of the elements, the troops persevered in their labors in the trenches. A heavy cannonade was kept up from the town, but with little effect. On the nineteenth the rain continued with increased violence. The troops were

without shelter of any kind, and the duties of the
siege were uncommonly severe.   In the evening
a spirited sortie was made by the garrison, in
which Colonel Fletcher the commanding engineer
was wounded. They were speedily charged back
into the town by the brigade of General Bowes;
after which the troops resumed their labors, and
continued to persevere in spite of every obstacle.
The loss on this occasion amounted to one hundred and twenty men in killed and wounded.   During the night of the twenty-first, the bridge across
the Guadiana was carried away by a sudden swell
of the river.   Owing to this misfortune, great difficulties occurred in bringing up the supplies necessary for the troops.   The only communication
was by a flying bridge, which could only be worked with great difficulty, and the quantity of provisions thus procured was found so utterly inadequate to the demand, that the most serious consequences were apprehended.   There were likewise,
other impediments to be overcome.   The trenches
on the low ground were flooded, and the earth became saturated with moisture.   To palliate this
evil, double working parties were employed in the
trenches.   Some with buckets, bailing out the
water, while others pushed forward the works.

By these extraordinary exertions, favored by a
change of weather, several batteries were completed on the twenty-fourth, and, on the following day, opened fire on Fort Picurina, which Lord

Wellington determined to carry by immediate assault. The attack was made by five hundred men of the third division, formed into three detachments. The right under the command of Major Shaw, of the the seventy-fourth; the centre under the Hon. Captain Powis of the eighty-third, and the left under Major Rudd of the seventy-seventh. Two of these columns advanced from the flanks of the parallel, and attacked the work in its gorge, while the third, consisting of one hundred men, under Captain Powis, escaladed the front, at a point, where the palisades had been much injured by the fire of the batteries. The latter soon succeeded in effecting an entrance, and a short but violent contest ensued.

The assailants and defenders were mingled in a confused *melee*, and the issue was yet undecided, when two columns, which had atttacked the work by the gorge, having succeeded, though with great difficulty, in effecting an entrance, appeared to the assistance of their comrades. This at once decided the issue of the attack. Of the garrison consisting of two hundred and fifty men, one officer and thirty-three men, alone escaped. The commander, three officers and eighty-six men were made prisoners, and the rest were either killed in the fort, or drowned in attempting to cross the inundation of the Rivillas. All the leading officers of the attacking columns were killed or wounded

and the total loss on the part of the besiegers exceeded two hundred men.

While the contest was going on in the fort, the
alarm bell was rung in the town, fire balls were
thrown up in all directions, and a random fire of
cannon and musketry was opened from every part
of the ramparts.   At the same time, a battalion of
the garrison made a sortie from the ravelin St.
Roque, but they were instantly driven back by the
detachment stationed to protect the attack.
Throughout the night a heavy fire was kept up
on the fort, which did little execution.   By the
capture of Picurina, the besiegers were enabled
to establish their second parellel with little loss,
and, on the night of the twenty-sixth, two breach-
ing batteries opened fire, within three hundred
yards of the body of the place.   On the thirtieth,
the fifth division under General Leith which Lord
Wellington had deemed it necessary to withdraw
from Beira, arrived at Elvas, and joined the camp
before Badajos.   It was now known that Soult with
his whole disposable force, was advancing to the
relief of the place ; and that Generals Graham
and Hill, the former of whom had pushed on to
Llevena were retreating on Albuera.   In the north,
Marmont having collected his forces took the advantage of the absence of our army, to cross the
frontier ; and masking Ciudad Rodrigo and Almeida, marched by Sabugal upon Guarda and Castello Branca, plundering the country as far as Covil-

had in the Sierre de Estrella. Our cavalry, which had been left to observe his motions, retreated towards the Tagus ; and a considerable body of militia under Generals Trant and Wilson fell back on Celorico. Under these circumstances, the operations of the siege were pushed on, if possible with increased rapidity; and, on the sixth of April, three extensive breaches having become practicable, orders were immediately issued for the assault. The plan of attack was as follows : General Picton, with the third division, was to make an attempt on the castle by escalade. Our division and the fourth, under Major General Colville and Lieutenant-Colonel Barnard, were to storm the breaches in the bastions of La Trinidada and Santa Maria, and in the connecting curtain. Gen. Leith with the fifth division was to escalade the rampart near the western gate ; and the left brigade, under Major-General Walker was to make a false attack on Fort Pardaleras, which he was to turn into a real one, should circumstances prove favorable. Brigadier-General Power, with his Portuguese brigade, was to threaten the *tete du-pont*, and the other works on the right of the Gudiana. At ten o'clock on the night of the sixth, our division and the fourth under General Colville and Colonel Barnard, moved out of the trenches, and advanced to the assault. From each company ten men were taken to precede the divisions as a forlorn hope. I volunteered as one of the ten

from my own company. On reaching the glacis
we were discovered by the garrison, and instantly
a tremendous fire opened. Though the carnage
in our ranks was very great, we continued our
advance, and entered the covered way at the points
where the palisades had been destroyed by the
batteries. Owing to the darkness of the night and
our attention being fixed on the fire of the enemy
we came unexpectedly upon the counterscarp, and
nearly half our party, myself among the number,
were precipitated into the ditch below. Much
bruised by the fall I lay a few minutes insensible,
till on the arrival of the main body, the ladders
were fixed down the counterscarp, and the descent
into the ditch was quickly effected.

Though the formation of the troops was necessarily broken in these operations, they immediately advanced against the breaches, and soon succeeded in gaining the ascent; but such were the
obstacles prepared by the enemy that it was found
impossible to surmount them. Not only had the
summit of the breaches been obstructed by *Chev-
aux de frise*, but deep and wide trenches had been
dug, in the bottom of which were planted iron
spikes, and the whole of the surrounding buildings
were casemated, and occupied by light infantry.
To overcome these obstacles many gallant but
unsuccessful attempts were made by our troops;
but after persevering with a courage impossible
to be surpassed, we were at length compelled to

retire. The attack was again renewed, but without more favorable issue ; and nearly all the superior officers being disabled, we were withdrawn to prepare for fresh efforts when the day should dawn. At the foot of the main breach leading on his troops, fell Sir Charles McLeod the colonel of our regiment, as brave a soldier as ever drew a sword. Twenty-one officers of the regiment were either killed or wounded, and of the ten men of our company who volunteered for the forlorn hope, only myself and a man by the name of Cumings came back alive, both wounded.

In the meanwhile the third division led by Gen. Kempt, and commanded by Gen. Picton, advanced to escalade the castle ; and on approaching the Rivillas, were received by a heavy fire from all the works to the eastward of the town. They speedily descended into the ditch and planted their ladders. These unfortunately were found too short, and did not reach within four feet the summit of the rampart. This obstacle, though not insuperable, materially diminished the rapidity of the ascent, and kept the troops longer exposed to a destructive fire, than would otherwise have been necessary. Showers of grenades, stones and rafters of wood, were likewise poured down on them by the enemy, and the slaughter was great. General Picton and General Kempt were carried from the field, severely wounded, and the command of the division devolved on Col. Campbell of the ninety-

fourth.   Under this officer the attack lost nothing
of its energy.   The troops, anxious to escape from
the dreadful fire to which they were exposed in
the ditch, eagerly mounted the ladders, and as they
reached the summit, formed on the rampart.   A
short struggle then ensued,—and in a few minutes
the division were in possession of the castle.   Soon
afterwards the brigade of Gen. Walker, after forcing the barrier on the road to Olivenca, succeeded in entering the town by escalade.   Before this
was effected, several of the ladders broke, and
General Walker was disabled by a severe wound.
The troops, however, persevered in the assault
with a spirit and gallantry which drew the ap-
plause of Lord Wellington, who witnessed their
efforts from a small eminence near the trenches,
from whence he directed the whole movements
of the attack.   The brigade of General Walker
then advancing by the ramparts, attacked in the
rear the troops posted for the defence of the
breaches, and immediately dispersed them.   No
sooner did Lord Wellington receive intelligence
of the success of the third and fifth divisions, than
he directed our division and the fourth again to advance on the breaches ; and fresh troops being
thrown into the town, all resistance ceased on the
part of the garrison.   General Philippon and his
staff, and about four hundred men escaped across
the river to Fort St. Christoval, and shortly afterwards surrendered.

The whole of the garrison, amounting nearly to four thousand, were made prisoners. A considerable number of arms and ammunition, one hundred and seventy-two pieces of artillery, and more than eighty thousand shot, were found in the place. The expenditure of life, on our part, during this extraordinary siege, was very great; by the returns the number of killed and wounded amounted to nearly five thousand. Considering the boldness of the effort, and the magnitnde of the obstacles to be overcome, the capture of Badajos is one of those events in their annals, of which Englishmen may well feel proud, "Never, probably," says Colonel Jones, "since the discovery of gunpowder, were men more exposed to its action, than those assembled in the ditch to assault the breaches. Many thousand shells and hand-grenades, numerous bags filled with powder, every kind of burning composition and destructive missile, had been prepared and placed along the parapet of the whole front; these, under an incessant roll of musketry, were hurled into the ditch without intermission, for upwards of two hours, giving to its surface an appearance of vomiting fire, and producing sudden flashes of light more vivid than the day, and the night was now light with the most dazzling fires, and now black with utter darkness." To complete the scene of horror, our troops on entering the town, committed debaucheries and excesses which required the greatest exertions of our commander to restrain; and it was not until he had made some severe examples, that the wild rapacity of his inflamed and elated troops began to abate. The men of our regiment were so intoxicated and given up to excess, that it was difficult to find sober men to bury the dead. At the request of our Major, I, with the assistance of another soldier, dug our Colonel's grave. We buried him on the top of the Powder-mill hill, outside the town.

Lord Wellington next advanced against Salamanca and directed his efforts against the fortified Convents in the neighborhood of that place. He had already with hot shot burned the Convent of St. Vincente, and having opened a breach in the gorge of the Forte Gajetano, the commandant hoisted the white flag, but demanded three hours delay before they surrendered. Our commander would grant only five minutes, and no submission being made at the expiration of that time, the batteries were re-opened, and the fort was taken at the bayonet's point. In the forts thus captured were found large quanties of clothing and military stores, and the whole garrisons in number about seven hundred men, were made prisoners of war. The forts had no sooner fallen than Marmont retired upon the Douro; and the hostile armies were now encamped on each side of the river. No movement was made by either for several days, till at length Marmont having concentrated his whole force passed the river; and by a forced march of forty miles, was on the 18th of July, in presence of our division and the fourth, who were posted on the Tratancos and formed the right of the army. Our situation was very critical. The enemy attempted to cut off our communication with the centre and left, and it was only by a resolute and successful charge of the cavalry, that we were at length extricated from our difficulties. On the twentieth, the two armies, amounting together to ninety thousand combatants, marched, for several hours together within half cannon shot of each other; but no attack took place. Nothing could be finer or more striking than the spectacle they presented, as they moved in parallel lines, in the most imposing order and regularity. The French General now grew impatient for battle, and on the twenty-first made an attempt to cut off our line of communication with Rodrigo. Wellington, who received the intelligence of this movement while at dinner, rose so hastily as to overturn the table, and exclaiming that Marmont's good genius had forsaken him, made immediate dispositions for the attack.

BATTLE OF SALAMANCA.

Before daylight on the morning of the 22d, both armies moved into position. That of our army extended from the Tormes to two steep and rugged heights, which, from their similarity, the na-

tives generally distinguished by the name of the
Sister Arapiles. The position of the French was
covered by a thick wood, and embraced the heights
of La Pena, and the hamlets of Calvarasso de Ari-
ba, and Calvarasso de Abaxo. In the morning a
great deal of skirmishing took place. Detachments from both armies endeavored to seize the
Arapiles heights, and the French succeeded in
gaining possession of the external and more distant one. The occupation of one of the Arapiles
by the enemy, occasioned some changes in the
position of our army. The right was extended *en
potence* to the heights behind the village of Arapiles, which was occupied by light infantry ; and
General Pakenham with the third division, and
Portuguese cavalry, was directed to cross the
Tormes, and take post at Aldea Tejada to lend
still farther support to the right flank. The morning passed in a series of manœuvres on the part
of Marmont, from which no conclusion could be
drawn with regard to his ultimate intentions.
Lord Wellington therefore contented himself with
keeping an accurate observation on all the movements of his adversary, ready at any moment to
assume the offensive, and equally so should sound
policy require it, to retreat. About two o'clock,
however, a sudden and decisive change took place
in the character of the enemy's demonstrations.
Under cover of a heavy cannonade, and a skirmish along the whole front of his line, Marmont

advanced his centre, making at the same time a movement to his left, as if intending to encircle the position of our army, and cut us off from the road to Ciudad Rodrigo. His line thus unduly extended, was necessarily weakened, and the favorable opportunity of attack thus presented, was immediately seized by Lord Wellington. The following was the disposition of the army at the moment of attack. Our division with the first, were on the left of the Arapiles, and formed the extreme left of the line. The fourth and fifth divisions were posted in a double line, in rear of the village of Arapiles, with the sixth and seventh divisions, and the division of Don Carlos d'Espana in reserve. On the left of the fourth division was the Portuguese brigade of General Pack ; on the right of the fifth, was that of General Bradford. The third division, with the main body of the cavalry formed the extreme right.

While these arrangements were in progress, the enemy made repeated attempts to gain possession of the village of Arapiles, occupied by a detachment of the Guards; but no important change took place in their general dispositions. The third division was then ordered to advance obliquely to its right, and turn the left of the position, while General Cole's and General Leith's divisions should attack it in front. The arrangments being completed, the third division, led by General Pakenham, moved on to the attack.

The division advanced in column of battalions, and was in the act of ascending the ridge occupied by the enemy, when the skirmishers were driven in by a large body of cavalry, who in a moment came sweeping along the brow of the ascent, on the right flank of the division. Fortunately the retreat of the light troops had given intelligence of their approach; and Colonel Campbell of the ninety-fourth, who commanded the brigade, had time to throw back the fifth regiment, *en potence*, which by a well directed volley, caused them to retreat indisorder.

General Pakenham no sooner crowned the heights on the extreme left of the French, than he formed line across their flank, and supported by General D'Urban's Portuguese cavalry, and some squadrons of the fourteenth, advanced towards the centre, carrying every thing before him. On every favorable point where they attempted to make a stand, they were charged with the bayonet; and with such vigor did General Pakenham follow up his success, that even the colours of our regiments were often seen waving over battalions of the enemy. Sir Stapleton Cotton with the cavalry charged the enemy in front, and cut to pieces a brigade of French infantry, though not without sustaining a severe loss in General Le Merchant, who was killed at the head of his brigade. The whole left wing of the enemy was now retreating in confusion, and above three thousand prisoners had been made by our troops. While the events just narrated were passing on the right of the army, the tide of success had not flowed with equal rapidity in the centre. The repeated attempts of General Pack to gain possession of the Arapiles height occupied by the enemy, were unsuccessful. On the retreat of the Portuguese, a body advanced from the height and made a gallant and very vehement attack on the flank of the fourth division, while warmly engaged with the enemy in its front. General Cole had been already wounded, and his division, disconcerted by this sudden attack, was compelled to retire in some confusion. The misfortune, however, was immediately repaired by the advance of a brigade of the fifth division, which by a change of front, took the enemy in flank, and subjecting them to a cross fire, forced them instantly to retreat. The fourth and fifth divisions then continued to advance, uninterrupted by any further reverse, and gained complete possession of the crest of the position. In the meanwhile the Arapiles was carried by General Clinton; and the third division had advanced from the left, along the centre of the French position, attacking and dispersing the enemy in every encounter. Marshal Marmont had had been wounded, and the command of the army devolved on General Clausel, who, with great promptitude and skill, now endeavored to rally his defeated troops in a new position, running nearly

at right angles with the original front. The
ground was admirably chosen. Either flank of
the position was supported by masses of cavalry;
and the artillery was so posted as not only to
sweep the whole face of the height, but to command all the ground in the vicinity. The assump-
tion of so strong a position caused a pause in the
movement of the troops. Lord Wellington having examined it, at length directed the fourth division to dislodge the enemy by a flank movement
on the left, while General Clinton's division, supported by the third and fifth, should attack it in
front. It was in this part of the action, that the
loss on our part was most severe. General Clinton's division, during the whole of its advance,
was exposed to a most destructive fire of artillery and musketry, which it sustained with the
greatest steadiness, till reaching the summit of
the height, it at once charged with the bayonet,
and the fourth division coming up, the enemy
abandoned the position in great confusion, and fled
towards Alba, where he crossed the Tormes. Our
troops continued the pursuit with great vigor, till
the approach of night, when the darkness and extreme fatigue of the troops, rendered it necessary
to halt. But for an unforseen circumstance, the
victory of Salamanca must have been attended
with even greater results. When the enemy took
up his second position, our division was directed
to march to Huerta, and the first division to Alba

de Tormes to cut off their retreat. On the part of the first division these orders were not executed, and the Spaniards having abandoned the castle of Alba on the approach of the French, the latter were enabled to effect their retreat across the Tormes without impediment.

The immediate results of this most splendid victory were the capture of eleven pieces of artillery, two eagles, and seven thousand prisoners. Three French Generals (Ferey, Thomieres and Desgraviers,) were killed; Marshal Marmont, Generals Bonnet, Clausel and Menne, were wounded. The total loss of the enemy cannot be calculated at less than fourteen thousand men. The number of killed and wounded on our part, was about five thousand two hundred, including six General officers, one 'of whom (Le Marchant) was killed, the others (Beresford, Leith, Cotton, Cole and Alten,) were wounded. The enemy taking advantage of the darkness, continued his flight during the night; and at day-dawn the pursuit was renewed on our part. The advanced guard, consisting of Major-General Baron Bock's and General Anson's brigades of cavalry, which joined during the night, succeeded in coming up with the enemy's rear division, strongly posted behind the village of La Serna. The two brigades instantly charged; and the French cavalry, panic-stricken by their recent defeat, fled in great confusion, leaving the infantry to their fate. The whole of the latter, consisting

of three battalions, were made prisoners. After
this disaster Clausel continued his retreat, by forced marches and in great disorder, towards Valladolid ; but evacuated this place at the approach
of Wellington, who pushed on to Madrid, and having forced the garrison to surrender, entered the
Spanish capital on the 13th of August, amid the
loud *vivas* of exulting crowds. The situation of
Lord Wellington now at Madrid, though brilliant
was full of peril. The defeated army of Marmont was still numerous, and had been largely
reinforced ; and a corps of observation of ten thousand men had been sent into Alava. The armies
of the south and centre, by forming a junction with
that of Suchet, might speedily advance against
the Capital, with a force at least treble in amount,
to that of our army. To remain in Madrid therefore was impossible, he therefore resolved to trans-
fer his operations to the north, and attempt the reduction of Burgos. On the 19th of September;
our army entered Burgos ; and the French under
General Souham, who, with a reinforcement of
nine thousand men, had arrived on the day previous, to assume the command, fell back to Brivi-
esca, leaving in the castle a garrison of two thousand men, under General Dubreton. On the evening of the nineteenth, a large horn-work, on a hill
called St. Michael was stormed and taken by our
troops. On the 22d at midnight, an unsuccessful
attempt was made to carry the outer, or escarp wall,

by escalade ; but on the 29th, a breach having been
made by the explosion of a mine, a party of the first
division attempted to storm it. They were, however, repulsed ; the lodgment was recovered and
the breach repaired ; and the besieged followed
up their success by making a sally, and gaining
possession of the trenches. Another effort was
made on our part on the 18th of October ; but, after a siege of thirty days, in which two thousand
of our troops perished, and which only failed for
want of the necessary means of attack, Burgos
was abandoned, and we commenced our retreat
towards Portugal. The retreat commenced on
the 21st of October, and was attended with great
difficulty and distress ; continual rain, deep and
miry roads, and a want of sufficient food, being
among the daily hardships which we had to encounter.

Under these circumstances, many irregularities
and excesses were committed by the men in the
course of their march, many of whom took to ma-
rauding for the purpose of obtaining food, whilst
others from exhaustion or indifference, lagged behind and fell into the hands of the enemy. Lord
Wellington on his arrival at head quarters, wrote
a letter, severely censuring the commanders of
the different brigades and regiments, which pro-
duced a powerful effect. During the retreat, Sir
Edward Paget was unfortunately made prisoner,
almost in the centre of our army. A detachment

of French light troops were concealed in a wood
on the road to Ciudad Rodrigo, and Sir Edward
observing an interval between the fifth and seventh divisions of infantry, rode alone to the rear to
enquire into the cause by which the progress of the
latter had been delayed. On his return he missed his
way and fell into the hands of the enemy. By
this unlucky accident, his country, at a moment
of peculiar need, was deprived of the services of
one of the bravest and most distinguished of her
leaders. On the 18th of November, the head quarters of Lord Wellington were at Ciudad Rodrigo,
and on the two following days, we crossed the
Agueda, and were distributed in cantonments,
where we were suffered to enjoy the repose necessary to prepare us for the toils of the succeeding campaign. During the long interval in which
we remained in cantonments no hostile movement
of importance took plaec.

On the 16th of May, 1813, the campaign opened.
Five divisions with a large force of cavalry, under
Sir Thomas Graham, who had resumed his station
as second in command, were directed to cross the
Douro, and effect a junction with the remainder
of the army near Valladolid, while Lord Wellington in person, with our division, and a brigade of
cavalry and a corps of Spaniards, moved towards
Salamanca, and Sir Rowland Hill with the troops
from Estramadura, was to advance on the same
point by Alba de Tormes. By these movements.

the line of the Douro was turned, in consequence of which, the defensive works of the enemy became entirely useless, and the whole of our army was united on the right bank of that river on the 3d of June. On the day following, Wellington, continuing his advance, compelled the French to evacuate Valladolid, and retire to Burgos, whither he pursued them, and forced them to abandon the place. By this movement, the enemy were driven behind the Ebro, which river our army passed, a few days afterwards without opposition. On the 18th our division came in contact with two brigades of French infantry, which we attacked and defeated with the loss of three hundred men. On the 19th Lord Wellington drove a French corps of observation from a strong position behind the Baygas ; and on the 20th, he collected all his divisions, and reconnoitered the enemy, who were now encamped at Vittoria, to the number of seventy thousand combatants, under the nominal command of Joseph Bonaparte in person, and determined on the following morning to attack him.

BATTLE OF VITTORIA.

Vittoria, the chief town of Alava, one of the Biscayan provinces, stands behind the little river Zadorra, in a plain about two leagues in extent, bounded on one side by a part of the Pyrenean chain, and on the other by a range of bold heights of

smaller altitude. The ground around Vittoria is
marked by considerable inequalities of surface, of
which the enemy did not fail to take advantage.
At the period in question, it was for the most part
covered with ripening corn, which gave conceal-
ment to the light troops, and sometimes even to
the movements of whole battalions during the engagement. The French army was posted as follows. The right extended northward, from Vittoria across the Zadorra, and rested on some
heights above the villages of Abechuco and Gamarra Major, covered by formidable field works.
Between the centre and right was a thick wood,
into which were thrown several battalions of infantry. The right of the centre occupied a strong
height commanding the valley of the Zadorra,
the bridges over which were fortified. It was
covered with infantry, flanked and otherwise
defended by one hundred pieces of cannon. The
advanced posts of the centre lined the banks of
the Zadorra. The left, and left centre crowned the
high ridge above the village of Subijana de Alava,
with a reserve posted at the village of Gomecha,
and a corps thrown out to occupy the bold mountains above Puebla, to protect the centre which
might otherwise have been turned by the main
road where it crosses the Zadorra. Thus posted,
the French army covered each of the three great
roads which concentrate at Vittoria, in the great
road to Bayonne. That of Logrono by its left,
that of Madrid by its centre, and that of Bilboa

by its right. It was commanded by Joseph in person, having Marshal Jourdan as Major-General. In point of numbers, there existed little disparity on either side, it having been found necessary before passing the Ebro, to detach General Foy with twelve thousand men towards Bilboa, to procure subsistence for the army, and keep in check the powerful guerilla bands which haunted the neighborhood; and General Clausel with a corps of fifteen thousand men was at Logrono. Lord Wellington likewise had found it necessary to employ the sixth division under General Packenham, in guarding the line of supply. The amount of combatants on either side, therefore may be fairly calculated at from seventy to seventy-five thousand men. At day light on the morning of the twenty-first of June, Lord Wellington put his army in motion in three great divisions. That on the right, under Sir Rowland Hill, consisting of the second British division, the Portuguse division of the Conde de Amarante, and Morillo's corps of Spaniards, was destined to commence the action, by attacking the enemy's left on the mountains behind the Subijana. The left column commanded by Sir Thomas Graham, composed of the first and fifth divisions, two brigades of cavalry, and the Spanish division of Longa, was directed by a wide movement to turn the enemy's right, and crossing the Zadorra, to cut off his retreat by the road to Bayonne. The centre corps, consisting of our division, the third, fourth and seventh, in two columns, was ordered to wait till both or one of the flank columns should have crossed the Zadorra and then to make a powerful attack on the French centre.

The Spanish troops under General Morillo, commenced the action by an attack on the enemy's corps posted above Puebla, supported by the light companies of the second division, and the seventy-first regiment, under the Honorable Colonel Cadogan. After a severe struggle, in which that most promising and gallant officer was mortally wounded, the enemy were driven from the heights at the point of the bayonet. Strong reinforcements were then brought up by the enemy, and the contest was renewed, and continued for some time, with great obstinacy on both sides. Sir Rowland Hill, however, having detached an additional force to support the troops already engaged, the French at length gave way, and yielded undisputed possession of the heights. Thus far successful, Sir Rowland Hill crossed the Zadorra, and directed two brigades of the second division to attack the heights of Subijana de Alava. Here the contest was severe. The troops advanced under a heavy fire of artillery, and succeeded in dislodging the enemy, and driving them back on their reserve. The heights thus gallantly carried, however, were too important, to be resigned, while a chance of regaining them remained. Fresh columns of attack

were formed, and repeated efforts were made by
the enemy to recover their ground, but without
success. At length Joseph, alarmed at these repeated failures, and the threatening attitude assumed by Sir Rowland Hill, withdrew his advanced posts from the Zadorra, and directed the left
to fall back for the defence of Vittoria. In the
meanwhile, our division and the fourth, under
General Cole, had passed the Zadorra at the bridge
of Nanclares and Tres Puentes; and the third
and seventh divisions, crossing by the bridge on
the Mendonza road, both columns advanced against
the height in the centre. At the same time, Sir
Rowland Hill moved forward from Subijana de
Alava, and vigorously followed the left wing in
its retreating movements. Though the enemy had
been forced to withdraw his left, the centre still
stood firm, and received our columns, advancing
from the Zadorra, with a fire so destructive, as for a
time to check our progress. Two brigades of horse-
artillery were then moved forward to the front;
and, thus supported, our centre columns continued
their advance in fine order. Notwithstanding the
difficulties of the ground, the division of Sir Thomas Picton first came in contact with a strong body
of the enemy, whom, by a spirited attack, he drove
into immediate retreat, with the loss of twenty-
eight pieces of artillery. On the approach of our
division with the fourth, the whole heights were
abandoned, and the French retired in admirable

order on Vittoria, taking advantage of every favorable position to turn on their pursuers. In the meanwhile, Sir Thomas Graham, with the left column, which on the evening before had been moved to Margina, was advancing by the high road from Bilboa to Vittoria. About ten o'clock, he approached the enemy's right, posted on the heights commanding the village of Abechuco. From these he immediately dislodged them, by attacks both in front and flank.

Having gained possession of the heights, Sir Thomas Graham directed General Oswald's division to advance against the village of Gamarra Major, which the enemy occupied in great force, while, with the first division, he attacked the village of Abechuco. Gamarra Major was carried in the most gallant style by the brigade of General Robinson, which advanced in columns of battalion, under a heavy fire of artillery and musketry, without firing a shot, and drove out the enemy at the point of the bayonet, with great slaughter, and the loss of three guns. The attack on Abechuco was no less successful. Under cover of the fire of two brigades of horse artillery, Colonel Halket's brigade of the German legion, advanced to the attack, and drove the enemy from the village, with the loss of three guns and a howitzer, captured by the light battalion in a very gallant charge. The village of Gamarra Menor was likewise carried by the Spaniards, under Longa, after a trifling resistance. During the operations at Abechuco, the enemy made the greatest efforts to re-establish themselves at Gamarra Major. A strong body advanced to regain the village, but were driven back in confusion by General Hay's brigade. In spite of this failure, another attempt was subsequently made; but Sir Thomas Graham having caused the houses in front of the bridge to be loopholed, and placed his artillery in a position to flank the approach, the enemy were again repulsed, and did not afterwards venture to renew the attack. Notwithstanding these successes, it was found impossible to cross the bridges, the heights on the left of the Zadorra being occupied by a strong reserve; and General Graham awaited the moment when the attacks on the enemy's left and centre should occasion the withdrawal of the corps in his front. This at length came. Towards evening, when the centre of our army had penetrated beyond Vittoria, the right wing of the enemy, fearing to be cut off, retired hastily from its position.

Sir Thomas Graham immediately pushed forward across the Zadorra, and took possession of the road to Bayonne, which, for some distance, runs along the margin of the river. Great confusion ensued. The baggage, heavy artillery, military chest, and court equipages of Joseph, had already been put in motion by that road, and were now intercepted. The enemy's columns, which

were also retreating on Bayonne, were forced back
into the Pampluna road; and in a moment the
French army became a vast mob, without organ-
ization of any sort, and divested of every attribute
of a military body. Never had any victory
achieved by the enemy over the rude and undisci-
plined Spanish levies been more complete; never
was any army reduced to a more absolute and total wreck, than that which now fled from the field
of Vittoria. Our troops pressed forward, allow-
ing not a moment of respite in which order might
be restored, and adding to the amount of our cap-
tures at almost every step. Unfortunately the
country was too much intersected by ditches, to
admit of the action of cavalry; and it was impossible for infantry advancing in military order, to
come up with an enemy who trusted solely for
safety to rapidity of flight. The amount of prisoners, therefore, was comparatively small, though
the pursuit was kept up with unrelenting activity
till the approach of night, when the extraordinary
fatigue of the troops occasioned it to be discontin-
ued. Joseph, whom from this period it would be
a mere mockery to designate as king, fled towards
Pampluna, and owed his safety to the swiftness
of his horse. The tenth hussars entered Vittoria
at full gallop, the moment after his carriage had
left it. Captain Windham, with one squadron,
pursued, and fired into the carriage; and Joseph
had barely time to throw himself on his horse, and

escape under the protection of an escort of dragoons.

The immediate results of the battle, were the
capture of one hundred and fifty-one guns, and
four hundred and fifteen caissons, with upwards
of fourteen thousand rounds of ammunition, nearly
two millions of musket cartridges, forty thousand
pounds of gunpowder, the military chest, and the
whole baggage of the army, including the baton
of Marshall Jourdan. Several carriages with
ladies, among whom was the Countess de Gazan,
likewise remained as trophies in the power of the
victors. Many other females of rank, whose hus-
bands were attached to the Court at Madrid,
sought safety by mingling in the confused *melee* of
fugitives. Being utterly unprepared for such a
disaster, their sufferings were extreme during the
retreat to the Pyrenees ; and many are stated to
have crossed the frontier barefooted, and in a
state of the most pitiable privation. Though the
defeat of the enemy was thus accompanied by
every conceivable concomitant of disgrace, the
loss of combatants on both sides was unusually
small. The amount of killed and wounded, on
our part, was less than five thousand. That of
the enemy is rated, by their own writers, as low
as six thousand, but was unquestionably greater.
The number of prisoners made by our own troops,
from the causes already mentioned, did not exceed one thousand.

This was the last battle in which I was engaged. We drove the French from Vittoria to the confines of their own country. On the day they crossed the lines, we had a sharp skirmish with the enemy. We then took up our position on the heights of Bara, or Vera, where we encamped and remained until the latter part of August.

On the evening of the 30th of August, the night previous to the taking of the town of St. Sebastian, I was placed as one of the advanced picket guard near to the outposts of the enemy. In the morning after the fog had cleared away we found ourselves surrounded by the French army.

Our regiment observing our position endeavored to rescue us.

After a severe contest, having fired all our ammunition away, we were overpowered and taken prisoners. We were hurried to Bayonne, where we remained till our army drove the French under the walls of that garrison.

At Bayonne we mingled with other prisoners, Spanish and Portuguese, who had been previously taken. From thence we were marched through France into Holland, and put in Jevet prison in the town of Susan. We were in all, five thousand and five hundred in number, and remained here, under good treatment, until the spring, when the Russians crossed the Rhine. The French being now alarmed at the advance of the Russians, fearing they might release us, divided the prisoners into detachments of five hundred each, and sent them for safety to different cantons in France.

My division, being the fifth, was sent to the town of Moines, where was an ancient guillotine, formerly the scene of cruelty and blood, during the French Revolution. As the Russians advanced towards Paris, and fought the battle of Troyes, we received orders to march to Tours, this latter place being considered more safe, and out of the reach of the allied forces.

While on our march to Tours, fourteen of my comrades, besides myself, having laid our plans the night before, deserted the guard, while on our line of march. We took French leave of our old keepers, while in a piece of woods, between Moines and Orleans. The Governor of the prison, apprehensive we might desert, as he knew the French were retreating before the Russians and Prussians, warned us while in the prison yard on the morning of our march, of the dangers and evil consequences of our attempting to run away. To all of which we turned a deaf ear. We had no arms of course, being prisoners, but we had received three days bread, a loaf to each man, which we thought would be sufficient to last, until we joined the allies. Our position on the march was in the centre, between the front and rear guard, which was composed of French invalids, all the effective men being required for active service.

There was a difference of opinion among us,

whether the guns of our escort were actually
loaded, some thought they were not, but it appeared to me that they had a shot in the locker in case
we attempted to leave the ranks. This actually
proved to be the case, for no sooner had we got into the woods than a smart volley came whizzing
round our ears, the effect of which we avoided by
covering ourselves on the retreat by the trees.

At this time the Russians and French were engaged, and we distinctly heard the sound of their
cannon, which served us as a guide to direct us to
the Russian and Prussian army.

On the second day about 11 o'clock, we arrived
in safety at the advanced posts of the Prussian
forces, where we were received with great cordiality. The Prussian commander sent an interpre-
ter with us to the Alcalde of the neighboring village, demanding of him in our behalf, a good dinner for each, and a bottle of the best wine. This
proved quite a treat to us after our poor fare, and
long imprisonment.

Shortly after this the allied army, moved forward and entered Paris, where I was requested to
become a waiter to an English officer, in the
Russian service, with whom I remained until
peace was concluded.

At the battle of Troyes, Bonaparte and his
whole army were discomfited. He with a remnant of his guards, took up a position, upon a
small conical hill, near Paris, where he surrender-

ed and was afterwards sent to Elba. I remained
in Paris about three months. This city is the
greatest place for crime and debauch in the world,
women and wine are as plenty as shad flies on
the Hudson.

Upon the exchange of prisoners I set out for
Dunkirk, in Holland, where I took passage on
board the King's cutter, and in a few hours landed at Dale. I went to Hyde and joined the 2d battalion of the 43d regiment, for my old and first
battalion lay at Bordeaux in France. Immediately after, an order came from the War Office, for ten
sergeants to join the Duke of York's Chasseurs,
a regiment then forming in the Isle of Wight. As
one of those ten, I volunteered, and joined that
regiment, and shortly we were ordered to the
island of St Vincent, in the West Indies.

I can now look back with gratitude on that pro-
tecting care that watched over my pathway from
the morning of childhood, protected my life, and
shielded me when in danger, while the bullets flew
around me like hail stones.

Had I when I left Paris, joined the first battalion of the 43d, my old regiment, I might, with
many of my brave comrades, have fallen in the battle of New Orleans, under the command of Pakenham, whose soldiers lay in heaps before the en-
trenchments of Andrew Jackson and his brave
Americans. Or had I survived and sailed with the
remnant of the British troops, from New Orleans,

to France, my bones might have lain bleaching
on the field of Waterloo.*

BATTLE OF WATERLOO.

The allied powers again took up arms for the
overthrow of Bonaparte, who had returned from
Elba; the Duke of Wellington having arrived
at Brussels early in April, was appointed field
marshal of the United Netherlands, the force under him amounting to eighty thousand, of which
about thirty-eight thousand were English. The
Prussians were already in Flanders, under the
command of Blucher; and the troops of Italy,
Russia and Austria, were also rapidly approaching the frontiers of France. Meantime, Napoleon
having been received with the greatest enthusi-
asm in his capital, had got together no less than
three hundred and seventy-five thousand men under arms, by the first of June; and on the 14th,
he appeared on the Belgian frontier with his army,
concentrated into three divisions, amounting to
one hundred and thirty thousand fighting men,
with a field artillery of three hundred and fifty
pieces. He had the utmost confidence in his
troops; and saying, as he threw himself into his
carriage to proceed to join them, " I go to measure myself against Wellington," set out from

* I was not in the battle of Waterloo, but for the benefit of the
reader will here insert a brief account of that memorable engagement.

Paris in full conviction of shortly returning to it as Emperor of France, and conqueror of Europe.

" Soldiers," said Napoleon, in his last address to his army, " this is the anniversary of Marengo, and of Friedland, which twice decided the fate of Europe. Then, as after the battles of Austerlitz and Wagram, we were too generous. We trusted to the oaths and protestations of princes, whom we left upon their thrones. Now, however, coalesced among themselves they conspire against our independence, and the most sacred rights of France. They have begun the most unjust of aggressions. Are not they and we the same still? Soldiers! at Jena, against these same Prussians, now so arrogant, you were as one to three; and, at Montmirail, one to six. Let those among you that have been prisoners in England, describe their pontons (the hulks), and tell the miseries they there endured. A moment of prosperity has united these senseless princes against us. The oppression and humiliation of France are beyond their power. If they enter France, they will there find a grave!"

Nothing could be more calculated than this address to inflame the passions and animate the courage of those to whom it was addressed. Impatient for battle, the French troops advanced rapidly to the Belgic territory; and, on the 15th of June, a body of them met the Prussian out-posts, at a short distance from the Sambre, and forced them to re-cross it with great loss. This success was followed up by the taking of Charleroi ; whilst a second body of the French,. advancing to Gosseiles, to intercept the Prussians who had evacuated the former town, were so electrified by the presence of Bonaparte, that, without waiting to fire a shot, they rushed furiously on their adversaries and drove them from all their positions.

Intelligence of this repulse reached the Duke of Wellington, at Brussels, on the night of the 15th, whilst he was at a ball, given by the Dutchess of Richmond. Without leaving the scene of festivity, where most of the British officers were also present, he gave orders for the route of march ; and at midnight, the whole city was suddenly awakened by the beat of the drum, and the sound of the trumpet summoning the troops to assemble. By eight o'clock in the morning of the 16th, all the regiments had quitted Brussels, and were marching upon Les Quatre Bras, where the Duke of Wellington, being strengthened with reinforcements under the Prince of Orange, assumed the offensive, and gave orders for the attack. His grand object was to maintain a line of communication with the Prussian troops, which the enemy, on the other hand, were as anxious to prevent, as on this point depended, in all probability, the ultimate fate of either army. The contest was furious, but decisive ; and terminated in the repulse of the French, who finding themselves suddenly exposed to solid columns of numerous battalions, supported by a formidable cavalry, which, until close upon them, had been concealed by uneven fields covered with high wheat and rye, appeared panic-struck, and fell back in dismay and confusion.

Marshal Ney was, however, little alarmed, expecting every moment the arrival of a corps of reserve, but which he now, for the first time, learnt, had been disposed of by Bonaparte elsewhere. " The shock," says Marshal Ney, in his letter giving an account of the battle to the Duke of Otranto, " which this intelligence gave me confounded me. Having no longer under me more than three divisions, instead of the eight upon which I calculated, I was obliged to renounce the hopes of victory ; and in spite of the intrepidity and devotion of my troops, my utmost efforts after that could only maintain me in my position till the close of the day."

In this dilemma, he ordered the eighth and eleventh cuirassiers to charge the first battalions, which they did with great bravery and captured one of the colours of the sixty-ninth regiment ; but the fire of the adverse infanty was so deadly and perpetual, that they were compelled to retreat in rapid disorder, and Wellington remained in possession of Quatre Bras.

In this action fell the brave Duke of Brunswick. But, notwithstanding the repulse of Ney,

Napoleon, before the close of the day, obtained his end, in separating the Prussians and the English, by the complete defeat of the former at Ligney, whence· he forced Blucher to retreat ; and that General having had his horse shot under him, only escaped falling into the hands of the French cuirassiers by the darkness of· the night.

Bonaparte now took possession of all the Prussian posts ; directed Grouchy to pursue Blucher with thirty thousand men ; and put himself in readiness to attack the English, whom he felt little doubt of overpowering. On the morning of the 17th, Wellington received information of the repulse of the Prussians, and of their retreat to Wavre ; in consequence of which he evacuated Quatre Bras, and retired by Genappe, upon Waterloo, where he took up his final position near the forest of Soigne. With the exception of an affair of cavalry, in which a corps of French lancers, after having repelled a charge of the seventh Hussars, were, in their turn, repulsed by the first regiment of life guards, no action of importance occured during the day. The approach of night was accompanied by a violent storm of rain, thunder and lightening, which rendered the bivouac of the troops wretched in the extreme : and tended rather to enervate than refresh them for the exertions of the forthcoming day.

During the night, Napoleon had, either from surmise or report, imagined that the British had retreated ; and on finding them still in their position, on the morning of the 18th, he is said to have exclaimed, in a transport of joy,—" I have them, then, at last, these English !"

Preparations on both sides now commenced for battle ; and by ten o'clock, the whole French army, with the exception of the force under Grouchy, was seen ranged along the heights opposite to those occupied by the British, amounting to about 80 or 90,000 men commanded by Napoleon in person. The army of the Duke of Wellington, consisted of about 70,000, which was so skillfully disposed that a great portion of it was entirely concealed from the enemy.

About noon, the first discharge of cannon was heard from the French lines, which was followed by a furious attack on the farm of Hougoumont, where a most deadly struggle took place, and which was so obstinately defended by the British, that the enemy set fire to the building, after having in vain attempted to drive their adversaries from the position. In the meantime, La Haye Sainte was the scene of a severe contest ; but it was at length carried by the French, after the most sanguinary action. The enemy now advanced towards Mont St. Jean ; and, as they approached, the English artillery made dreadful havoc in their ranks ; but they persisted in the attack with unflinching bravery, and with an enthusiastic perseverance, which indicated that they had decided on this ground as their grand point of concentration for victory or defeat. The roar of the cannon, the shouts of the soldiery, the hissing of balls and grape shot, and the explosion of shells, now mingled together with an awful effect; the enemy gained ground, though slowly, and one of their columns drew near to Mont St. Jean. " At the same time," says a French officer, in his account of the battle, " our cavalry rushed to carry the guns on the plains, but was charged, in its turn, by the enemy's horse, who issued in a body from the hollows where they had lain in ambuscade, and the slaughter became horrible.

Neither side gave way one step. Fresh columns reinforce them ; the charge is repeated. Three times the French are on the point of forcing the positions ; and three times they are driven back. " In these assaults," says the same authority, " Lord Wellington exposed himself very much; and, in order to direct in person, the efforts of his troops, several times threw himself into the midst of the melee, to animate them by his presence." He moved about in every direction, giving his orders and encouraging his men in the midst of the hottest fire ; and, at one time, perceiving the fifty-second and ninety-fifth regiments waver and give ground under the attack of an overwhelming force, he rallied them, placed himself at their head, and exclaiming, " We must not be beaten ;—what will they say in England ?" Charged in person and

turned the fortune of the day. At this moment
the issue of the contest was doubtful; the British
ranks, although they had suffered much, were unbroken; but great confusion, it is said, prevailed
in their rear. However no appearance of trouble
was visible in their front, which sustained the furious attacks of the French with such firmness and
obstinacy, that they in their turn began to lose
somewhat of their confidence and impetuosity.

It was now seven o'clock, when a general officer informed Bonaparte, who still kept ordering
fresh troops forward, that his soldiers would be
annihilated by one of the batteries if they continued in their present position; at the same time re-
questing to know what they should do to elude its
destructive fire. Carry it, said the Emperor. At
the same time, he kept sending off despatches to
Paris, exclaiming to his Secretary, in a tone of
distraction, " Above all, fail not to say the victory is mine."

At this time two bodies of Prussians, which he
mistook for Grouchy's, coming up, opened an attack on Bonaparte's flank and rear.

Lord Wellington now gave the signal for a general advance; to meet which, Napoleon, as his
last and only hope, led on his imperial guard.
These old warriors entered the plain with their
accustomed intrepidity, and courage was restored
through the whole line. The guard made several
charges, but was constantly repulsed, crushed by

a terrible artillery that each minute seemed to multiply. The French grenadiers, however, still kept their ground; and whilst they beheld the grape shot make day-light through their ranks, destroying at the rate of a hundred and fifty men in a minute, promptly and cooly closed their shattered files, and remained firm and immoveable. But their intrepidity was of little avail or duration; a charge directed against their flank threw them into disorder, and the cry of " all is lost,—the guard is driven back!" was heard on every side. In an instant the whole French army confused, fled,—pursued by their enemy. Napoleon narrowly escaped being taken prisoner by secreting himself in a cider orchard, near the farm of Caillon.

Thus ended the memorable battle of Watterloo, in which nearly 40,000 combatants perished.

After remaining a year or over at St. Vincent, we received the rout for the island of Jamaica; our company was stationed at Fort George, Fort Antonio, on the east end of the island. During our stay in this Fort we were much afflicted with disease, especially with the vomito and yellow fever. Sixty-two of our company died. Here I was confined to the hospital for three months.

At the reduction of the army, in the year 1819. my regiment, which was the last formed, was ordered to Quebec, where we were disbanded.

Each private received from the British government a grant of land in Upper Canada of one hundred acres and a year's provisions.

Being a Sergeant my grant was two hundred
acres, but I never saw the land nor availed myself of the Royal bounty. These grants were forfeited in 1843.

A year ago, while at the Crown office, in Montreal, at offer was made to me of one hundred
acres, in consideration of my former services as a
soldier in the British army.

It was in Montreal, I first contracted the appe-
tite for strong drink. There were pipers and fid-
lers in almost every low tavern! Here I was
shorn of my strength, or more properly speaking
of my money; and when at last I thought the
Philistines would be upon me, I bid farewell to
the city, and in company with several others,
sought for employment on the government works
at Long Soult, on the Grand River. In this place
I staid but one month, and left for Potsdam in the
State of New York, where I spent the winter, as
a waiter in a *Hot-hell* (Hotel), or one of the Dev-
il's wigwams, as they are better termed. Here
I studied the drunkard's system of navigation, and
had many a hard cruise in the sea of intemper-
ance, in which my frail bark was well nigh foundered.

As moderate drinking is the great high-way,
By which all drunkards pass'd the other day,

Supremely blind must all their followers be,
Though here and there an inverted track they see.
In vain death packs the drunkards in his urn—
No sooner gone, the tiplers drunkards turn,
Ere thou art snar'd—cease tampering with the foe,
Nor in the way of death and ruin go.
Come give your pledge, from tipling to abstain,
Embrace the temperance cause and safe remain.

I worked the summer of 1820, in Utica, on the canal. The allowance of seven gills of grog a day, on these works was not very favorable to the cause of temperance. Most of the men drank very freely. There were however two young men, brothers, from the north of Ireland, protestants, who could not be prevailed upon to taste a drop, and never had from their youth up.

In the fall of this year, I went into an Auction store in Utica, and laid out my money in goods and commenced pedling. I took the road and travelled north, until I entered Vermont. Here I had my pack stolen.

I afterwards settled in the town of Berkshire, in Franklin County, Vermont, where I worked on a farm, for a man whose name was Francis Rublee. I here became acquainted with the family of my wife, whose name was Gray. Mrs. Gray, whose daughter I afterwards married, was a kind hearted pious woman, and took all opportunities to persuade me to become a christian. I was first brought under serious impressions, by hearing Mrs. Gray read a tract called the Shepherd of Newton Stewarts. I soon after began to read the bible, and commenced going to meeting. My convictions increased, as light broke into my mind, for several months, when one morning as I was praying for mercy, in a sequestred spot near the house, I found peace and pardon through faith in Jesus Christ. I then joined the praying army, and for the first five years, I ran in the way of God's commandments ; but alas! the glory soon departed, for I became entangled with the yoke of bondage, by indulging too freely in the intoxicating bowl.

I found now by sad experience, that he that knoweth his master's will and doeth it not, shall be beaten with many stripes.

I sought the Lord and he heard the voice of my supplication, and restored once more to me the joys of his salvation, and I again found pleasure in his service.

Upon reflection, I can now see, that had I never been persuaded to read the bible, I should in all probability have found a drunkard's grave. But I thank God that he ever snatched me as a brand from the burning, and from the fires which the cursed bowl kindles on the drunkard's vitals while on earth. Upon the death of my father-in-law, being defrauded of the property, that came by the right of my wife, I removed into the State of New York, where I have resided ever since.

In the year 1841, when the great Temperance reformation commenced, I entered the ranks of the teetotal army as a Lecturer, and for the last six years have travelled the greater part of the time in various parts of New England and New York. Wherever I have been engaged in this good cause, I have been received with the greatest cordiality, and have seen many drunkard's reclaimed and restored to their friends to usefulness and society.

I take this opportunity of expressing my gratitude to the friends of the temperance cause in general, for their kindness, and for encouraging me in my weak efforts to promote the best interests of my fellow men ; hoping to witness before I die the complete triumph of the glorious temperance reformation.

If God spares my life, I shall still continue to exhort and encourage the poor drunkard to cast away the unhallowed bowl, and to bear in mind that all the danger lies in the first glass.

There is no safety for moderate drinkers; the only sure way is to touch not the inebriating cup. It is an old saying, that "drinking water will neither make a man sick nor in debt, nor his wife, (if he has one,) a widow.

> Make room for the thousands on thousands returning,
> From the desolate pathway of darkness and sin.
> Their hearts for the accents of kindness are yearning,
> Oh! shout in your gladness and welcome them in.
>
> From the isles of the ocean, the vallies and mountains,
> With the proud flag of victory, in triumph unfurld.
> They come to partake of the life giving fountain,
> Those waters are flowing to gladden the world.

Oh, stlll at our posts we stand to deliver,
'Till the light burns again on each desolate heart,
And the demon of drunkenness is vanquished forever,
Whose breath, like a plague spot has darkened the earth.

In conclusion, may the star of Temperance in union with the star of Bethelem, lighten up the dark horizon of this benighted earth.

Also published in facsimile in *The Spellmount Library of Military History* and available from all good bookshops. In case of difficulty, contact Spellmount Publishers.

THE MILITARY ADVENTURES OF CHARLES O'NEIL by Charles O'Neil
Introduction by Bernard Cornwell

First published in 1851, these are the memoirs of an Irish soldier who served with Wellington's Army during the Peninsular War and the continental campaigns from 1811 to 1815 Almost unknown in the UK, as the author emigrated to America straight after, it includes his eye-witness accounts of the bloody battle of Barossa, the memorable siege of Badajoz – and a graphic description of the battle of Waterloo where he was badly wounded.

ROUGH NOTES OF SEVEN CAMPAIGNS: in Portugal, Spain, France and America during the Years 1809–1815 by John Spencer Cooper
Introduction by Ian Fletcher

Originally published in 1869, this is one of the most sought-after volumes of Peninsular War reminiscences. A vivid account of the greatest battles and sieges of the war including Talavera, Busaco, Albuera, Ciudad Rodrigo, Badajoz, Vittoria, the Pyrenees, Orthes and Toulouse and the New Orleans campaign of 1815.

THE JOURNAL OF AN ARMY SURGEON DURING THE PENINSULAR WAR by Charles Boutflower
Introduction by Dr Christopher Ticehurst

A facsimile edition of a rare journal written by an army surgeon who joined the 40th Regiment in Malta in 1801 and subsequently served with it in the West Indies, South America and the Peninsular War. Described by his family 'as a man of great activity and a general favourite with all his acquaintances', he saw action from 1810 to 1813 including Busaco, Ciudad Rodrigo, Badajoz and Salamanca – gaining a well-deserved promotion to Surgeon to the staff of Sir Rowland Hill's Brigade in 1812.

RECOLLECTIONS OF THE PENINSULA by Moyle Sherer
Introduction by Philip Haythornthwaite

Reissued more than 170 years after its first publication, this is one of the acknowledged classic accounts of the Peninsular War. Moyle Sherer, described by a comrade as 'a gentleman, a scholar, an author and a most zealous soldier', had a keen eye for observation and an ability to describe both the battles – Busaco, Albuera, Arroyo dos Molinos, Vittoria and the Pyrenees – and the emotions he felt at the time with uncommon clarity.